Local History

A Handbook for Enthusiasts

G.M. Hibbins, C. Fahey and M.R. Askew

George Allen & Unwin
Sydney London Boston

First published in 1985
George Allen & Unwin Australia Pty Ltd
8 Napier Street, North Sydney, NSW 2060 Australia

George Allen & Unwin (Publishers) Ltd
Park Lane, Hemel Hempstead, Herts HP2 4TE England

Allen & Unwin Inc.
Fifty Cross Street, Winchester, Mass 01890 USA

National Library of Australia
Cataloguing-in-Publication entry:

Hibbins, G.M. (Gillian Mary), 1936– .
  Local history.

  Bibliography.
  Includes index.
  ISBN 0 86861 756 3.
  ISBN 0 86861 764 4 (pbk.).

  1. Australia—History, Local—Sources. 2.
  Australia—Historiography. 3. Local history—
  Technique. I. Fahey, C. (Charles). II. Askew,
  M.R. (Mark R.). III. Title.
994'.007'2

Typeset in 10/12 Times by Graphicraft Typesetters, Hong Kong
Printed in China by Bright Sun (Shenzhen) Printing Co. Ltd.

Contents

Appendixes

Tables

DIAGRAMS

Illustrations

Preface

In these years of historical anniversaries and celebrations, many people who are not professional historians seek their own or their community's past. An amateur, says the dictionary, is one who does something for the love of it. This book is designed to help lovers of history try their hand at researching and writing history. The text warns of possible problems, instructs in historical etiquette, and encourages the savouring of delights along the way. It makes no pretensions to philosophising. The authors all earn their bread and butter—mainly bread—in researching and writing the history of people and places. Our experience lies in having fallen into more historical pits than most—and clambered out—and in times close enough to remember. We offer here our hard-won knowledge of historical sources and how to use them.

Local historians have the opportunity to contribute to Australian history by doing careful and precise research in a restricted area. They can, for instance, describe methods of work and ways of life which have generally disappeared, and research local reactions to Australia-wide events such as the nature of Aboriginal resistance, the community's response to conscription, the employment of women during the 1930s depression, or the experience of selector, soldier settler and postwar migrant. We hope to encourage you to set your work within the larger scene. This would have a double benefit, adding significance to small-scale research and depth to wider understandings. It means making connections, relating a school to a community, a family to an industry or to changing social and economic movements, a town to its hinterland, and a linking of the work of both professional and amateur, a development all lovers of history would applaud.

Although this book in the main uses Victorian examples—because the authors happen to have done most of their work in Victoria—its methods and advice are of course for people working anywhere in Australia. We hope that people from all over Australia will join enthusiastically in the chase.

We would like to thank Dr Marian Aveling for her help, and Venetia Nelson for her editorial work. We gratefully acknowledge the contribution of the following people and institutions in providing illustrations: the Archives Authority of New South Wales, Frank Campbell of the Geelong West Timber House Museum Project, the City of Waverley, the Department of Crown Lands and Survey in Victoria, the Mitchell Library in Sydney, the Monash University Geography Department, the National Library of Australia, the Public Record Office of Victoria, L.A. Schumer, the Springvale Historical Society, and the Victorian Tourism Commission. The existence of this handbook has been due to the financial support of Victoria's 150th Anniversary Celebrations 1984–85.

1

Introduction to research

More and more people are discovering that researching history can be fun and that there are all sorts of topics which offer scope for some probing of the past. Research has the addictive excitement of the chase and the satisfaction of cornering the quarry. It provides the companionship of fellow hunters and the enjoyment of comparing notes. The nice thing about history is that it encompasses life in all its facets, and can lead one in a multitude of fascinating directions. Irrelevant byways can seduce the unwary; if you have the time, then enjoy the dalliance. The catch, however, is the qualification—'if you have the time'. Anybody who has tried historical research knows very well that just keeping to the path you wish to pursue can be time-consuming—and its end elusive. Historical researchers can spend almost as much time discovering where information is not as finding where it is. The result is like an iceberg—the fraction which shows above the water surface does not indicate the great mass of effort supporting it. Although this book aims to help you reduce the unprofitable amount of time you could spend in research, be warned that history takes time.

Be realistic about time

For this reason, if you are engaged on a project which must have time limits, such as a history essay, or research for a historical anniversary celebration, or a family reunion, it is essential to set realistic goals. Young students in particular may choose a topic on which research has been done over three or four years and little discovered. What hope then does the student have in three or four weeks? It is a project doomed to finish in extreme frustration and despair, not to mention low marks. The other extreme is almost as bad. The subject has been so well researched that there are numerous books and articles on the subject, or vast stacks of dusty files, minutely written diaries, volumes of fragile newspaper print or reels of eye-exhausting microfilm. To do justice to the subject will take years of your life, years you are not prepared to devote as you like to play tennis, window-shop or read a good book, as well as do some historical research.

A reconnaissance?

For students, one possibility is that you may be able to come to some agreement with your teacher that you do what is called a reconnaissance of the topic and present this as part of your work or as a full alternative to your research project or paper. In a reconnaissance, you make plain what you aim to discover and then detail the steps you have taken to achieve that aim. If you look through an index, visit a map collection, or check a local newspaper for photographs, but have no luck, then you can explain this. In this way the work you put in which turns up nothing at all, or very little, can be noted, and the time expended, which in the ordinary course of events would go unwritten and unremarked, can receive some credit. Not all sorts of material are available to student researchers; some societies and institutions have been forced to restrict access to protect the material. Your teacher may be prepared to reward a genuine attempt at research even if the information gained is little, or the work falls short of the required number of words. In this sort of approach, it is the learning about historical method which is important and this may be preferable to rehashing somebody else's work, a common position people fall back on.

Speculate with words

Whatever kind of historical research you are about to begin, there are two immediate points to keep in mind. First, to proceed successfully you need to be prepared to experiment with words. Catalogues and indexes are cross-referenced so that under 'bees' you will also find 'see honey, honey plants', but you will not find 'see insects, eucalypts, wild food, stings, self-sufficiency'. That sort of free association you have to supply yourself, and while you may not consult a catalogue necessarily under those headings, you might know of a book that 'could have something on that'. Be adventurous with spelling—that of other people's anyway—particularly with names. A family called Keys turned up in the shipping records under Kais! (And it is just as well to try Australasian as well as Australian when looking for the Builders and Decorators' Magazine or whatever.)

Similarly it is good practice when you take notes to observe carefully the spelling you meet. Place names change over time and these changes are sometimes a help in determining their origin, for example, Parnham (Aboriginal name for waterhole)—Baungan (first squatter's misheard name for run on same waterhole—Bangan (common spelling)—Bangholm (new squatter's name for homestead on sandy ridge on same run)—Bangholme (Melbourne suburb). It is part of historical accuracy to use people's names correctly. If you come across somebody's signature then, unless he or she is obviously illiterate, this should be taken as definitive and will remove doubt about whether a letter should be doubled or not or whether a name starts with Mc or Mac.

Taking notes

Second, most researchers tackling a project of some length use the tried and tested method of writing notes on the index cards. These can be easily carried, come in different colours (for different subjects), and can be filed and reordered as desired in a shoebox. They should of course be of the same size. Use separate cards to note details of each source and make only a brief source reference to each on the card on which you take the note. Do, however, take a full and accurate note of the date if working from a newspaper. Keep separate cards for separate notes. Do not write on the back unless the note carries over from the front of the card. Distinguish your own comments and cross-references from that of the note by some consistent device, [square brackets perhaps] (see p. 4).

SOURCES

Armed with your willingness to experiment with words, and your pile of cards, you can now search for your sources of information.

Secondary sources

Begin with the card catalogue and microfiche catalogue of a library and look for what is called the 'literature'. This consists of the writing already done by people on the subject: the books, articles, theses, etc. These are also called the secondary sources because they are *interpretations* of the past written at a later time. They will give you an idea of the current state of knowledge about the subject in which you are interested. If the literature is vast, you may want to scale

subject of the note

summary of information

'quotation from text'

... indicates omission of irrelevance from quotation

source reference to another card which holds full details of title, author, date, etc. and location

[cross ...

[own supposition]

[own clarification]

date

page reference

circa (about)

Aboriginal deaths - Bangerang tribe
Between Delangen [Edward River]
and Goulburn R. signs of large number
of deaths but not of smallpox.
"It is evident a terrible mortality
has swept them [the Aborigines] in
numbers away for ... there are
burial places in every sandhill,
three of them contained upwards
of fifty graves ... Many of the
graves appear to have been only
recently [tenanted]."
Sturt Journal p.24   14 June, 1838
[See also Curr, E. 1883: suspects severe
mortality c 1790 from smallpox]

down your subject and refine it to a more manageable size. If there is no literature at all, you may consider the possibility that this is a very elusive subject to research, and widen your scope.

On the other hand, it may be that the subject is one which nobody else has yet bothered to research and you will be the first to venture in. For instance, you want to write a short biography of a writer, or the history of a school, or an essay on cabinet-making in Australia. If there is no literature directly relevant, there may be books or articles which border on the subject, an account of the literary group in which the writer moved, a history of a nearby school, or a book on Australian timber. They may well carry a bibliography (a list of works consulted) which will lead you to other sources, or footnotes which bear more directly on your concerns and can be followed up.

Reference books

Encyclopaedias contain essays summarising individual topics; these can be used as an introduction to a topic about which you know very little—a starting point. *The Australian Eycyclopaedia*, for example, deals with a number of subjects: a delve at random shows Repatriation followed by Reptiles, Repulse Bay, Edmund Resch (brewer), Reserve Bank of Australia, Responsible Government, Retail Trade, and Returned Servicemen's organisations. There are several editions and early ones should not be neglected as they can carry good articles which in later editions are not so comprehensive on an earlier period.

Encyclopaedias belong to another class of books which will help you—reference books. A **handbook** is designed to provide facts on one broad subject with a leaning towards respectable and generally accepted information rather than the latest research. *A Handbook of Australian Government and Politics, 1890 1964*, by C.A. Hughes and B.D. Graham, for example, provides information on such matters as governors, ministries, portfolio lists, electoral law and years of elections. A **yearbook** is essentially a handbook containing current information on the main political, social and economic developments, with some statistics, of the year concerned. Past issues may therefore be useful. There are yearbooks for each State and for Australia as a whole. **Almanacs** attempt the same information, but the range of subjects is so wide in an almanac that the treatment is necessarily lacking in depth. **Chronologies** or Books of Dates list and describe historical events concisely and without analysis. They may be useful for summaries of major legislation. They provide a context both in Australia and overseas in which to place a particular event.

They may also provide quick checks on information given in secondary sources. Australians are only just starting to produce this kind of reference.

Although **atlases** are useful in the usual way, that is, to look at physical features, places, natural resources and climatic conditions, there are also specifically historical atlases depicting explorations or events in a particular area over time. Historical maps of Australia are included in general atlases rather than meriting an atlas of their own, but one was published for Western Australia's 150th anniversary, and one is being produced for the bicentenary of 1988.

Subject dictionaries help the reader to understand the specialised words which each academic discipline uses as a form of shorthand among its practitioners, such as the 'donkey vote', which in politics means a vote marked 1–2–3–4–5 straight down a ballot paper, or the common words which have a restricted use in politics, such as 'division', a term used to describe the formal method of determining a vote in parliament. Of particular use to historians are dictionaries of geology, geography, political science, biography, place names, education, and of course history.

There are also dictionaries which give the history of words. Words change in meaning over time, such as 'squatter' which came from denoting a man who occupied land illegally to signifying a large landowner. They change from country to country, such as 'lagoon', which in England referred to a salt or brackish pond separated from the sea by a low sandbank but in Australia was used for freshwater ponds formed by a creek or spring. There are books on the Australian idiom, which are helpful if one is to understand phrases no longer used, such as 'lambing down' (fleecing an agricultural labourer of his cheque in a pub) or words like 'fizzer' (a wild horse), 'clinah' (girl or female sweetheart) or 'corduroy' (to bed a road with logs to make it passable in wet weather). There are expressions to do with land settlement, such as 'dummying' (the practice of taking up land illegally on behalf of somebody else) or 'peacocking' (buying the best part of a piece of land and thus making the rest unattractive to others). Such dictionaries will explain 'emu-bobbing', 'crab-holes', 'a cocky', 'a dog-leg fence', 'sandy blight', and a hundred other expressions you may meet in reading your sources.

Finally **indexes** are used mainly to find journal articles on specific topics and are particularly important becaue the articles are often more recent than the information found in books, or so specialised that they would not find a wide enough audience to be worth publishing as a book. One such is T. Hogan et al., *Index to Journal Articles on Australian history* (Armidale: University of New England, 1976). **Abstracts** will give a short summary of the contents which allows the researcher to decide whether it is worthwhile chasing up a full article, especially if it means getting a book from a distant library through an interlibrary loan.

Primary sources

Primary sources are the important sources for the historian and provide the essential basis for research. 'Research' in this context means a scholarly investigation of a subject in order to increase our knowledge of it, and not just a collection of other people's views on the same matter. Primary sources are those which came into being during the time the historian is researching. They usually comprise material written at the time but are certainly not limited to this: they could just as usefully be buildings, paintings, clothing or anything else, just as long as they took form during the time under study. The importance of a primary source is generally distinguished by its closeness to the action. For this reason, **manuscripts** take pride of place, for handwriting implies a close, immediate association with the matter. Printing words is more formal and more mannered than the less governed, less inhibited act of writing. Moreover, printed documents are sometimes copies of handwritten accounts, and anything which is copied is open to error, as writers and printers sadly acknowledge. H.F. Gurner in his *Chronicle of Port Phillip* published in 1876, wrote of 'a station at Dandenong called Bigning, water-holes adjoining, a station which Mr. Alfred Langhorne had formed'. Fortunately we still have the papers of the informant, J.C. Bourke, who had in fact written 'a station at Dandenong called "Bigning Waterholes", adjoining a station which Mr. Alfred Langhorne had formed'. The placement of one comma and the addition of another makes the difference of two stations instead of one; nevertheless Gurner's printed words have mislead local historians on this matter for over one hundred years.

Official documents are second in importance. These are often the result of inquiry and, ostensibly at least, some effort to eliminate bias and preserve integrity has been made. **Private documents** are considered to be less constrained by these efforts and to be much more likely to be the result of individual viewpoints. Consider, for instance, the likely difference in the response you would expect to the same event in a politician's diary (manuscript), a Royal Commission's report (official document), and a newspaper editorial (private document).

Last in the hierarchy of primary sources are those which contain some secondary aspect to them. They are usually further away in time. These include **contemporary histories** such as those of the 1975 constitutional crisis in Australia, reminiscences such as Andrew Crombie's *After Sixty Years: or Recollections of an Australian Bushman*, or an autobiographical work such as A.B. Facey's *A Fortunate Life*. Such works give information about the times the writer studies or recalls and in some cases are more useful for what the author unwittingly conveys to the reader of the opinions and values belonging to the era in which he is actually writing, commonly held attitudes to Aboriginals, women, work, sex, death and so on, more difficult to glean than descriptions of events and people.

Many handwritten documents have been published. These vary from the letters of Victorian pioneers, written in reply to Governor La Trobe's request for information on the days of early settlement and edited by T.F. Bride (1898), to John Hawdon's *Journal of a Journey from New South Wales to Adelaide undertaken in 1838* (Melbourne: Georgian House, 1952).

Some primary documents have been collected and published, sometimes with some secondary editorial comment. They provide archival material inaccessible for most people and include cartoons and photographs, as well as letters, official documents, excerpts from diaries and so on. *Historical Records of Australia* and *Historical Records of New South Wales* are examples; there also collections of documents by historians C.M.H. Clarke and F.K. Crowley. Such documents are tidied up and lack the often revealing trivia scribbled on the actual documents held in the archives.

Archives

It is only in the last couple of decades that historians have come knocking on the archivists' door. Archives are the records held permanently because it is expected that they may be of some value in the future. They are chosen from the written documents or other sorts of records created in the course of the activities of a government, a semi-governmental agency, a private organisation or an individual, and which are no longer needed. The word 'archives' also refers to the place in which these records are kept, although 'repositories' is sometimes used to distinguish the place from its holdings. Commonwealth Government archives are kept at the Australian Archives Office in Brighton, Victoria, and are generally available to the public once they are 30 years old, although some are restricted for longer if they touch on sensitive areas. Some organisations such as churches, schools and large business firms keep their own archives. Others contribute their papers to libraries and university archives; these archives may build up a specialist reputation, for example of having a good collection of records of land companies or trade unions.

Archivists keep the papers they receive in their original order, however disorganised that may be. The keys to individual information are the ones used when the files were current; they may be file registers, subject indexes or lists. Archivists try to understand the individual system used in actual practice by the department or corporation which created the records before listing the records and describing them. It is a massive job and one which has been done brilliantly in some areas and not at all in others.

If you are lucky, you may find in the archives all sorts of material bearing on your research, for records contained anything useful to the organisation, and that could be photographs, maps, newspaper clippings, blueprints, even samples, as well correspondence between ordinary people and the organisation. Administrations want answers to their problems and they send out questionnaires and commission surveys. They seek figures—how many are needed of a service or product, how many times a year, for how many people, at what price, and so on, lots of statistical data for the historian to compile and use. On the other hand, you may find that everybody knows that such-and-such a file, the one you badly need, exists, but nobody, nobody, can find it.

Some much used archival material, such as shipping records, has been microfilmed, and this practice will increase. Both sides of a piece of paper are put on microfilm, for much interesting material is written in the margin or on the folded back edge of a page by a clerk or official in the course of making a decision. When you are looking at a microfiche it is not easy to work out whether the two pages which follow each other are separate pages in fact, or back-and-front, a dilemma which does not exist when you can handle the actual pages. This may be important if you need a date, and it could be misleading if you assume back-and-front when it is actually two different pieces of paper.

Much potential archival material still exists with organisations or in the hands of past officials. Such material ranges from the records of a shire to the minutes of a kindergarten or the accounts of a progress association. These records require a lot of work to go through: unless you are researching that particular organisation, or have already to hand particular dates which are important, they are probably best left for the professional historian. In the meantime a move to establish some local archives, discussed with the historical society or library, could well save the records of the local Guide movement, or the now defunct cycling club, from a bonfire.

Interviewing

Rather more fun is talking to people about the past, or if you prefer, 'oral history'. Oral history is not meant to replace written sources but to add yet another way of acquiring information. It can amplify the pieces between the bald statement in the minutes: 'After considerable debate, it was moved and seconded that the association sell the hall. Motion passed' and the closing note: 'The chairman offered his resignation which was accepted with regret'. This amplification is as it should be. People doing research tend to rush off and ask somebody the dates when the hall was sold and when the chairman resigned, only to be suitably rewarded with time-blurred inaccurate memories, when both pieces of information can be obtained correctly from titles, rate books or minutes. What you cannot get from these documents is why these decisions were made and if there is a connection between the two. Though the memories of these events may be coloured by strong emotions stirred by some bitter dispute, you need to talk to the committee members if possible and, after making careful allowance for prejudices and considering all your information, try to explain what happened. So do not talk to people for factual detail such as dates unless you want a rough lead to the likely time, but for the sort of information you simply cannot get anywhere else, the off-the-record stuff, by which is meant the generally unremarked fabric of day-to-day living.

There are some good manuals on oral history giving practical advice and examples of questions to ask. Articles on the place of oral history and its disadvantages and advantages have been published in books on history. If you are set on doing some interviewing, read them.

Interviewing should be left until you have a good idea of what you are talking about. This goes back to the point just made. It is not the factual framework you seek but the detail, the sort of bits and pieces which give life and noise and texture to theory and facts. But you must have the theory and facts first. At the practical level you simply will not know what your interviewee is on about if you do not share the same background of information, and you will not ask the pertinent questions or know which answers are the important ones to pursue.

Moreover, your interviewees may well be irritated by your inability to understand the background they know so intimately, unless of course it concerns some skill or profession about which you wish to learn, in which case they may be flattered by the implied teacher–student relationship. Thus the farmer raising chickens will be happy to tell you what he puts in poultry mash, although he has done it every day for years. That sort of information is best obtained in interviews because it is so hard to get elsewhere, and little things which are foreign to your own upbringing or sex are easily explored in talking. For example, the farm couple will explain rust in wheat, the workings of a whim, swing-gates, churning butter, and why bullocks pulled loads better than horses (they are more flexible around corners and therefore better in timbered country).

All this depends on establishing a rapport, which is basically having the tact and friendliness to set another person at ease. That is not hard because you are genuinely interested in what is being said, the essential for any successful conversation. But there are techniques. Guided questions will prevent meandering reminiscences on aunts and football matches, but a mechanical sortie through a rigid list will not win unguarded asides or the unsolicited red herring which you never suspected could prove so flavoursome. A relevant photograph may bring a more complete and precise response than you might get otherwise. Read the books on practical tips. Analyse the good interviewer's technique on television—he has done his homework and strives for rapport.

If you are having a tape transcribed to paper, make sure you get it all. Typists can emasculate the whole feel of an interview by cleaning it up as they go, simply by removing the hesitations, if nothing else.

Local legends

Local legends should not be dismissed out of hand; they usually have a grain of truth in them somewhere. It is often the researcher's unwelcome task to separate legend from likelihood, sometimes stripping the story of its glamorous aspects in the process. Take comfort: it takes more than fact to stop a good story. Legends acquire a life of their own and may have a significance of their own, if one can only discern it. In research on a Melbourne suburb, for example, the name of Marcus Clarke was constantly evoked. It was there the celebrated author had written *For The Term of His Natural Life*, it was asserted, and a Marcus Road and a Clarke Road were cited as 'proof'. The names could be ascribed to an enterprising estate agent but they still testified to some sort of presence. Moreover a long-lived inhabitant remembered his father having some dealings with Clarke. The researcher was puzzled. None of the secondary sources mentioned Clarke living in the district; on the contrary, they wrote of him living elsewhere. The first real piece of evidence that an association existed lay in the Shire rate books which showed Clarke paying the rates, or rather neglecting to pay the rates, on his cousin's property in the district. Finally a letter reproduced in a biography (B. Elliot. Oxford, 1958 p. 179) provided a solution. Clarke had been acting as an agent for his cousin's property near Melbourne on which Clarke had 'built a shooting box of six rooms. There is a fine orchard and plenty of game. Two or three people go with me [from Saturday night to Monday morning] and we spend the time pleasantly.' Although the biographer had not been able to identify the place, the probability that this letter applied to this particular property seems high. Unfortunately the letter was written after the publication of his famous novel, but the real point of interest here is the question why has this association of a man with a place, originally brief in time, continued for over 100 years? One can only speculate—Clarke's own charisma? Or a desire for reflected intellectual glory in a suburb not noted for its percentage of inhabitants with higher education? The need for some sort of local hero, however momentary?

Pictorial sources

There can be few countries in the world where the early settlement by the white man has been so well illustrated. From its beginning all aspects of the new and strange land were drawn and painted, and many **early illustrations** were reproduced in quantity by **woodcuts, engravings** or **lithographs**. These were made by drawing on to a woodblock, or a copper or steel plate for an engraving, or a limestone block for a lithograph, inking the drawing and then printing out copies. Some were fine works of art used to illustrate books and newspapers. Today we have copies of these reproduced photographically as prints, which from the historian's point of view, as opposed to the collector's, are as valuable as the originals.

Usually they show views of the countryside, of Australian life, of the Aboriginals, and of the flora and fauna. Explorers' journals are illustrated by the artists who were taken along for the specific purpose of bringing back a pictorial record of the journey. Sydney Parkinson, the principal artist for the naturalists on Cook's voyage to the south on the *Endeavour*, made nearly 1000 drawings of animals, fish, birds, insects, reptiles, including some inaccurate sketches of the kangaroo. He died on the homeward journey, so that not all are complete: most would have been finished with the help of his colour notes and pressed specimens on his return to England. There are also about 100 drawings of native boats, inhabitants and coastal landscapes which are important for people interested in what is called 'contact phenomena', that is, matters relating to the first meetings of the indigenous people of the south seas and Europeans. Parkinson's

1 A cautionary tale: this steel engraving of alluvial gold washing is taken from E.C. Booth's *Australia Illustrated* published in London in 1874, which attributes the engraving to S. Bradshaw and the original artwork to John Skinner Prout. Art historians maintain that many of the engravings in Booth's book are copied from lithographs made by Prout in the 1840s while he was in Australia. But Prout returned to England before the gold rushes, so presumably for this particular picture he either imagined the scene or used other artists' work as a basis. Rex Nan Kivell Collection, National Library of Australia.

drawings provided the basis for many of the copper engravings which did appear after the voyage thanks to Joseph Banks. The French scientific voyages published in Paris between 1807 and 1855 include many fascinating engravings and lithographs of the Australian coast and its plants and animals. Many Australians would be acquainted with the prints of Samuel Taylor Gill's lively lithographs of the Victorian goldfields and G.F. Angas's of South Australia in the 1840s. Gill and others, such as Terry, Wilmore, Booth, Troedel and von Guerard, made lithographs of Sydney, Melbourne and the Australian landscape. As the century progressed, photographs were reproduced as woodcuts, engravings and lithographs: they were often panoramic views popular in supplements to newspapers.

Photography became popular in the 1850s, but it was mainly studio photography; since it was necessary to develop from a glass negative while it was still wet, outdoor work was difficult though not impossible. Outdoor backgrounds, for instance in posed collections of

2   This vigorous lithograph by Samuel Thomas Gill entitled 'Arrival of Geelong mail, main road, Ballaarat', was published in *The Diggers and Diggings As They Are in 1855*. For the local historian it provides detail of contemporary housing, transport and clothing as well as the idea that the arrival of the mail was something of an event. National Library of Australia.

Aboriginals, were mocked up in studios. In the 1880s the development of a dry-plate process allowed much more freedom to photograph in the great outdoors, and further improvements in printing from photographs began the age of the postcard at the turn of the century.

Picture postcards are useful for the twentieth century, the earliest begin vignettes of views around Sydney dating from 1898. Many, of course, were topographical, featuring cliffs, rivers, waterfalls, mountains and so on. Much topographical information is incidentally provided in pictures of bridges, weirs, boats, experimental farms, timber-cutters, and so on. Buildings range from hotels, lighthouses

3   This photograph by J.W. Lindt was published in *Album—Australian Aborigines*, Grafton, c. 1875. The painted backdrop, silver-birch mia-mia upright and studio floor planks throw doubt on the authenticity of the appearance of the weapons, native baskets and the crescent shaped king-plate worn by one of the Aboriginals. King-plates were given by the British, ostensibly to honour the leader of a local group, probably to both flatter and placate an influential Aboriginal. National Library of Australia.

and town halls to bandstands, army barracks and forges. Some postcards feature specific events such as parades, strikes, markets, or disasters—floods, mice plagues or dust storms. Industrial and agricultural scenes reveal land use by details of the haystacks, farm machinery, sawmills, goldmines, and bullock teams. Postcards are now sought after by collectors, and shops which sell them may be a source of some help.

Pictorial illustrations provide a wealth of detail which written descriptions usually do not include because a writer assumes such details are known to his reader. These may be everyday tasks of occupations now obsolete such as the blacksmith's; they may be signs, vehicles, dress, goods for sale in shop windows, vegetation or the state of the road. For the sympathetic viewer, pictures may offer a feel for the place at different times which is hard to gain in other ways—by evoking perhaps the heat, the dust and the struggle of life.

State libraries, university libraries and some local libraries hold picture collections, visual documentation of the history of the country, in differing degrees of accessibility and progress of cataloguing. Melbourne's La Trobe library, for instance, holds nearly 50 000 items including paintings, prints, photographs by all the major photographers, architectural drawings, posters and an extensive range of postcards.

The National Library of Australia has been acquiring a pictorial collection for its informative value, and has now about one quarter of a million photographs. Most are stored in compactus shelving, filed and indexed. They can be readily viewed and copies obtained. Although each photograph is only filed in one place, it might be relevant to a number of subjects so that it is cross-referenced. Nevertheless viewers seeking an illustration of a particular subject should think laterally about other subject headings under which it could appear. For example, somebody with an interest in military uniforms should not only look under 'army' but also under 'celebrations'.

Most historical societies will have a small collection of newspaper clippings with pictures, photographs by local residents, a few postcards and perhaps a calendar with hand-drawn pictures advertising local stores. Photographers with a long-established suburban practice may be worth enquiries (see also aerial photographs p. 42).

---

4   This postcard has a December 1903 postmark on the reverse side. The Boer war concluded in May 1902 so the photograph was taken between these two dates, probably in 1903. The Postcard Collection, State Library of Victoria.

Souvenir from Stawell.

Just to send hearty good wishes for the Xmas season & New Year from E. J. Davies & family

A. Picard Stawell   Central Park, Stawell, Victoria

The gates are erected in memory of the Stawell boys who went to the War.

ASSESSMENT OF SOURCES

Some research workers like to plunge straight into reading the primary sources because they value reaching directly to the contemporary material without the interposition of a second person's words, preferring to make their own interpretations unhindered by another's viewpoint, values or vision. This takes longer and it may cover much ground already tilled, so it can be sensible to read the secondary sources, with a stalwart scepticism, and then read the primary sources.

Bias and fact

The question of historical bias, selectivity, assumptions and values is, at worst, a cold war of verbal mud-slinging and, at best, a philosophical discussion of the highest order. It is sufficient here to distinguish between some of the different kinds of historical statements that you will come across in your efforts to reconstruct the past. One should not underestimate the difficulty of this undertaking; when you think of the problems involved in sorting out the cause of yesterday's road accident, then it is not hard to appreciate the complexity of deciding what happened in the past.

Some factual statements can be agreed upon. That Robert Menzies was born on 20 December 1894 would not be disputed as long as everybody was agreed that the Robert Menzies in question was Robert Gordon Menzies, once Prime Minister of Australia. More complicated statements may be supported by reliable evidence and be generally agreed upon, for example: most Cornish emigrants to Australia went to South Australia and most were miners. Statements about motivation and cause, however, are complex and produce debate. The British government's prime motives for founding the colony of New South Wales have been the subject for intermittent contention since 1952, with different historians plumping for its establishment as a convict destination, or a South Pacific trading port, or a source of naval supplies, notably flax and timber for Britain or India. Such interpretations are supported, and the alternatives assaulted, by the best primary evidence each can muster. The controversy seems likely to continue as historians seek further information.

During the last two decades the traditional methods and assumptions of historians have been increasingly attacked, and this has been beneficial in producing new approaches and a fresh appreciation of the uncertainty of historical generalisations. There has been a move to research the lives of common people as well as the elites. Women's history, Aboriginal history and urban history have all developed. This has meant winkling out of the scanty evidence some part of the lives of the inarticulate, helped by some new methods of enquiry such as techniques from sociology and statistics, the use of the computer, and analysis of photographs as evidence. Most history is revised at some stage, but an appreciation of this should not prevent anyone from trying to research the past and write about it.

Judging what you read

Assessment of your source is an essential part of making a historical judgment or interpretation. In everyday conversation, the speakers make constant mental assessments of the reliability of what they are being told, making adjustments for what they know of the speaker and of the subject matter. There are people we know who are coaxers, romancers, con men, hypocrites and leg-pullers. On the receiving end are those who are gullible and naive—who lack critical assessment. Most of us have developed this alertness to some degree, but, for some reason, tend to drop our guard with the written word. Essentially, however, the process is the same.

You need some knowledge of the writer. Does he or she understand the subject? Are these the words of a farmer talking about crops, or is this a tourist speaking? How long has this person lived here? For instance, Charles Fraser gives a detailed account of the Swan River and Cockburn Sound during the exploration of the HM *Success* in 1827. How reliable is that description? Fraser appears in the *Australian Dictionary of Biography* (vol 1. p. 416), from which you can discover that he was the Colonial Botanist of New South Wales and generally highly regarded. He had been in Australia for over ten years and travelled extensively in that time. Presumably because of this familiarity with the Australian terrain and flora, he would have been less prejudiced by the novelty of the vegetation and more able to appreciate its subtleties than newer arrivals with eyes less accustomed to the landscape. So historians have been happy to accept the account, although some difficulty with the botanical names arises (see p. 53). On the other hand, you might treat Paul Strzelecki's account of his exploration in Gippsland in 1840 with some reservation, having read Henly's biography (*ADB* vol. 2, p. 494). While recognising Strzelecki's achievements, Henly is not unaware of the discrepancies between what Strzelecki said and did: his unautho-rised use of the title 'Count' was perhaps indicative of the man.

The same question of expertise arises with secondary sources. Has the writer academic qualifications or practical experience? How long has the researcher been in the field? Does length of time make the expert more experienced or, alternatively, less receptive to the latest ideas? How serious is the author about the work? A look at the footnotes, bibliography, blurb on the author, and the date of publication should help to answer such queries. If you are well informed on part of the subject matter, read the author on that, and if that seems to have been presented accurately, then the chances are that the rest will be all right also. But keep checking, especially if you meet conflicting statements.

You should also try to identify the source's bias. It may be consciously slanted, perhaps to promote a cause, whitewash an offensive event, attack another person, earn promotion, favour or money, and so on. In pursuit of these aims the writer may lie. He is more likely to distort the truth by omitting some aspects of it or by unduly emphasising others. Unconsciously we all have some sort of slant because we consider certain things to be important, and our writing reflects this; it could not do otherwise.

Can you trust the figures?

Figures can be even more intimidating in their authority than the written word. Statistical knowledge is the branch of mathematics concerned with the collection and analysis of data (numerical facts) and the drawing of conclusions from the information collected and analysed. But the same questions apply. What is the source of the figures? Who was the compiler and what was or is his bias? Who analysed the figures and how would this interpretation be biased? Statistics are wonderful providers of patterns—those generalisations about life which tell us what percentage of people did what—which is why professional historians are trying to learn this time-consuming and expensive expertise and how to present the information without mystifying or boring the reader. You can venture into this field by following the information given on elementary demography in chap-ter 3. There are numerous problems. The first lies in the collection of data—how carefully was this done? Second, cause and correlation should not be confused. Because two events occur at the same time, or follow one another, it is not necessarily true that one causes the other. A statistical association is not the same as showing cause and effect. Get competent advice if you compile your own figures.

Can you believe your eyes?

Visual perception of a landscape is influenced by the cultural background of the viewer. The European settlers took time to appreciate the vast size of the new land, the quality of light and the subtlety of Australian flora and fauna. They yearned for the deciduous trees and the distinct difference in the seasons.` This is reflected in early colonial art: what is presented is neat, carefully cleaned up, doll-like, in other words, Anglicised. It is impossible to tell what the trees are; they look like romanticised saplings of indeterminate genera from some verdant stage play.

An appreciation that events of historic significance were taking place meant that artists were asked to record them, but the results were more often of artistic worth than of historical accuracy. Some pictures were done at the time of the event, such as William Strutt's annotated sketches of the opening of the first Parliament of Victoria on 13 November 1851, but others were done at a distance, both in time and place. John Longstaff's *Arrival of Burke, Wills and King at the Deserted Camp, Coopers Creek, Sunday evening 21 April 1861* was completed in 1906 and painted in England. Longstaff relied on sketches he had done in Port Augusta for the landscape and is said to have modelled Burke on a London tramp. Its virtues as a picture obviously do not lie in providing the historian with help. Others were purely the figments of imagination showing perhaps the meeting of famous people who never knew each other. The draughtsman working from a photograph could add buildings and people to his lithograph if he wanted to, and some did. Nevertheless the illustrations in nineteenth-century newspapers are another source of great fascination for the historian despite the constant need to crosscheck.

Photographs have the virtue of being less vulnerable to the distorting view of the artist, but what is being photographed is still dependent on the personality of the person pointing the camera. The mere choice of topic is open to suspicion: most people tend to photograph the unusual rather than the typical. If you are relying heavily on a photograph or series of photographs for evidence, it is important to find out as much as you can about the photographer, why he is taking the photographs and who is paying for them. Such information is not easy to get, so photographs are best used to suggest possible lines of enquiry to be tested against other sources.

Is it authentic?

Assessment of sources is irrelevant if the document is not authentic, that is, not what it purports to be. Fraudulent documents bedevil the historian overseas, but fortunately the authenticity of a document has so far not been an issue in Australia: its time may come. Remember the excitement and controversy which arose in 1983 over the 'Hitler Diaries', an affray in which an eminent British historian supporting their authenticity had his reputation sadly diminished when they were dismissed as forgeries. Imagine the interest, and offers of dollars, that would be aroused by the 'certain discovery' of the remains of Leichhardt's expedition (which disappeared in 1848) and his manuscript diary and sketchbook, or of letters sent home by a Chinaman at Ballarat in 1854 who witnessed the Eureka Stockade rebellion, or of Governor La Trobe's notes for an account of his Australian experience which he planned to write called 'A Colonial Governor', a project halted by his failing eyesight.

How is authenticity judged? Mainly by a feel for the 'rightness' of a document as belonging to its time, as shown by its likely existence, language, terminology, handwriting, and type of paper. Most historians rely on their knowledge and experience to pick something out of place or anachronistic, but a serious inquiry into a document would call on technical expertise.

A trap for beginners can be maps in secondary sources. They may be reproductions of originals. They can also be redrawn copies of originals, or they may be drawn by the author to illustrate where he or she thinks various features existed. A historian learns to pick the difference, but some readers tend to regard all maps as having the same authenticity. The source of a map should be explained in the caption. If this is not given, then it should be treated with suspicion.

THE USE OF SOURCES

Because the type of source and the assessment of that source's reliability is such an important part of the historical process, anyone writing history should supply a record of their sources for those who follow them. This is true even if it just means giving the references for a record of the family tree or for the written notes of the talk given to a historical society meeting.

Footnotes

The best way to do this is to footnote. People who write articles and theses know how to footnote, and there are plenty of books around which show you how to do this correctly. However it is not necessary to have footnotes full of 'ibids' and 'passims' if you find this a bore. Footnoting is like having good manners: one does not need a book on etiquette to know that the essence of good manners is to make the people around you feel comfortable. The point of footnotes is to set out your source of information so that other people can find it or assess its reliability should they wish to do so. When you think a footnote is necessary, place a number at the end of the phrase, sentence or paragraph that contains the information to be documented. Then at the end of the page or at the end of the written material you can add the source. You may end up with something like this:

---

1   Mrs P. Jones (my aunt) Glenelg, Adelaide, South Australia, personal letter, 3/4/83
2   Birth certificate of Anne McDonnell from New South Wales Registrar of Births and Deaths
3   *Memoirs of a Stockman* by Harry Peck published in 1942 in Melbourne
4   Mr L. Nottingham, resident Wagga Wagga since 1917, conversation 14/8/77
5   Rutherglen Shire Rate Book for 1887 held by Shire.
6   Postcard of footbridge and vehicle ford, Four Mile Creek, c. 1910, in Wattle Valley Historical Society Collection, Tasmania.
7   Headstone, grave of E. McPherson, North Point Cemetery, Queensland.

In this fictitious example, the letter and the conversation cannot be readily checked but at least the reader would have the derivation of your information. The birth certificate, memoirs, rate book, postcard and grave could all be followed up if a researcher was interested. And of course, add your name and the date to your manuscript because you will be a source too and may end up in somebody's footnote!

---

1   Reader, A., *Talk to Historical Society*, MS, 1984, p. 3

For the same reasons, if you quote from a source, quote *exactly* and if you have to leave some of it out, indicate this with three full stops (see the sample index card on p. 4).

Take care of the sources

When that somebody gets around to checking the source you have in your footnote, she likes to find it in the same good condition as you found it. In other words, take care of your sources when you use them. This means more than obvious things such as not removing pieces, or using the papers as coasters for your coffee mug, but turning fragile pages gently, not writing your notes with the source as backing, and using a pencil instead of a biro to take notes (a rule in most libraries and archives). It means carefully noting the spot in a box from which you took a file and returning it to that *exact* place. It means not upsetting the order of the file itself.

Archaeologists plead for anybody making a 'find' not to pick it up, but to contact the relevant Ministry for Conservation or nearest Lands Department. It is now against the law to excavate for Aboriginal relics without a permit, nor can they be bought or sold. If you do discover some historical item of interest or value, get expert advice before you try to restore it. Better still, resist the temptation to keep items you come across and so avoid the possibility that their past will be lost once you are no longer around to provide it. Label them carefully and give them to a museum. Do return the letters, photographs, catalogues or whatever else you may be trustingly lent. Offer any pictorial material to your local society or State picture collection. They will happily copy it and return the original to you.

Go to the library prepared

The custodians of the various libraries, archives, government departments and historical societies at which you seek information are usually helpful and patient. But it is not possible to give everyone a personal introduction to research in a particular area, so it is important to educate yourself before you go to such a place. Most institutions now have some sort of handout which gives relevant information. The fact that you are reading this book shows that you realise the importance of such an approach; nevertheless because you will only get the fullest response from your contacts if you go prepared, this point deserves emphasis.

Before approaching an archive for government records on a particular subject, take into account the way archives were formed. A file was created to deal with a specific situation. This needs some creative thinking—what situation could have acted as a catalyst for the formation of a file relevant to your subject matter, and what Government Department or agency might have been involved in that situation? That may give you a starting point. Commonwealth legal and financial matters have remained since Federation with the Attorney General's Department and the Treasury, but the transference of functions and reordering of departments, especially recently, makes for archivists' ague. The various current functions of each Commonwealth Department and a concise history of each appear in the *Commonwealth Government Directory* available from the Government Publishing Service. So think in the order: subject—function—department or agency—original register or index—record. Any knowledge about the historical structure of the organisation whose records you seek helps, but the process is still a bit like trying a dive with two somersaults and luck off the high tower.

Read up the background

Obviously the more Australian history you know, the more it helps. At least read an outline of the period in which you are interested. This will prevent the simplest of mistakes, as in the church history which begins with the selling of its suburb's land before the area had in fact been explored—and the date was not a printer's mistake either! Knowledge of Australia's economic depressions and booms and the whereabouts of gold strikes may help to explain why Uncle Harry suddenly left for Western Australia in 1893.

You may need to know the relevant local government boundaries, and these change over the years. 'Local government' as a term refers to the councils which administer some 900 local districts in Australia. These districts vary from small, thickly populated urban areas to larger rural units, are called by different names such as borough or shire, and have a variety of functions. See the article in the *Australian Encyclopaedia*. The rural shires are generally divided into 'ridings' and the urban units into 'wards'; these are electoral divisions for the local Council and they also change. Council rate books are divided into ridings or wards because the ratepayers vote within the area in which they live or own property. The right to vote in such elections is another matter which has changed, so that electoral rolls before a certain date, depending on your State, will only include property owners.

You cannot research satisfactorily in a vacuum. Find out about the education system before you tackle a school, land legislation before you look at land files, the religious background to a church. The weather loomed large in the fortunes of our forebears, so you need to know where you can get accurate information on your part of the world. As a sort of rough guide to disasters, there were major floods in many parts of Australia in 1863, 1867, 1870, 1875, 1887, 1889–94, 1910–11, 1916–17, 1929–1931, 1949–50, 1954–55, and 1974, but major droughts in 1864–66, 1880, 1886, 1888, 1895–1903, 1911–16, 1918–20, 1940–41, 1944–45, 1946–47, 1957–58, 1965–66, 1967–68 and 1982–83.

Decimal currency and metric measures

The introduction of decimal currency in Australia in February 1966 and of metric measures in the early 1970s have given historians a mid-cipher crisis and brief flirtations with a calculator. A general consensus has emerged, however, which is not to meddle with the two systems. Translating one into another side by side with one in brackets, as in 19 531 083 acres (7 904 938 hectares), has been tried but found to be a clumsy method of dealing with the problem. Certainly there is some merit to leaving pounds, shillings and pence intact. At the time of conversion, one pound (£) or twenty shillings was equal to two dollars ($). Since then inflation has distorted this, a process which has equally undermined the validity of comparing prices in 1850 and 1950 even if they were in the same currency. It seems cheap to buy an acre of land for £2, but not when you know that a stockman and his wife were getting £35 a year at the same time. Converting acres into hectares may appear to make more sense, but decisions based on imperial measurements had an internal consistency of their own, for instance, the squatter's pre-emptive right (see p. 34) was designated as 640 acres or one square mile, and many surveyed crown allotments as 160 acres or one-quarter of a square mile. To translate 640 acres into 259 hectares and 160 acres into 65 hectares obscures the reasoning behind the choice of those original figures. It may be of some help to translate the occasional figure, such as points of rain into millimetres, or Fahrenheit temperatures to Celsius, and miles to kilometres for future readers, but the continuous use of modern measures outside the time of the text, more so in narrative than in analysis, has the unharmonious effect of anachronism. Each writer must make his own decision on that. Today most historians avoid converting sums of money over time, and both decimal currency and metric measures are used only after the date of their introduction.

Dating photographs

Most pictorial illustrations can be, and have been, dated accurately, but local photographs and postcards may need some research.

Annotations on the back should not automatically be accepted as correct, for you have no indication when such a note was made or the circumstances which prompted the note. Few of us conscientiously date our own photographs when we get them back developed. We know we should. There is little secondary literature on types of postcards or the firms and photographers who issued them. Your best hope is the postmark or a date included by the writer in the message on the reverse side, although these only indicate that the photograph was taken earlier—but probably not much earlier. Otherwise it is a matter of detective work. An identification of the process by which the photograph was made will give you the earliest possible date. Dress is an obvious help; for example, bustles had taken over from crinolines and ties from cravats in 1870. There are reference books on Australian fashions and military uniforms you can consult. Electric light poles, or the lack of them, may be a starting point if you can establish when electricity arrived in the town. The size of trees provides an estimate of the passage of time in a comparison of photographs of the same site. Enlargements of photographs reveal intriguing details, some of which may help dating. A shop window, for instance, might show an advertisement for that week's 'talky' at the local picture theatre and that can be checked in the local newspaper.

Never date a photograph or postcard in any official way on a guess, even an educated guess, as it can be accepted uncritically. Narrow down the likely range of dates as well as you can and explain briefly how that range was deduced. Your explanation may read as follows:

> 'This photograph of Main Street was taken between 1911 and 1917. It is known from the rate books that Robinson took over the store from White in 1911 and Robinson's name appears in the sign over the door. The donor of the card, Mrs Brent, tells us that the man in the doorway was her uncle John, and he died fighting at Passchendaele in 1917.'

Chances are that some car buff will write to tell you that the car photographed in the street was not imported into Australia until 1915, and you can narrow the gap a bit more. At the very least, if you must go for a date and you are unsure, use the device of writing c. before it (c. 1914). This is Latin, 'circa', meaning 'about' or 'approximately'. Sometimes the abbreviation ca is used for this.

Taking photographs

Photocopying has made taking a copy of much written information for record or display a comparatively easy, cheap and convenient process. There are occasions, however, when you may want a photograph of a document or of a picture, and this can be expensive. Photographs for reference can be taken adequately with almost any 35 mm single-lens reflex camera with a built-in light meter using fast film. The most practical is a camera which will focus down to 33 cm (thirteen inches) or less. To take a closer picture, perhaps of a specific part of the subject matter which, enlarged, might reveal information too small to be seen on the original, a close-up lens attachment is necessary for the less complicated camera and extension rings for the more sophisticated. Sometimes such information can be had merely by taking a slide of the material and projecting it on to a screen, thus automatically enlarging it.

The flavour of the past

Some things do not change—people still fall in and out of love, get drunk, cry, gossip, conspire, laugh, play practical jokes, fight and comfort each other—and so one can in many ways try to step back into the past. Try to imagine filling a 200-gallon tank with a bucket from a river, attending church by the flickering light of jam tins filled with fat and a rag wick, keeping meat without a refrigerator, being on one end of a crosscut saw at the bottom of a large-boled red gum and patrolling a levee bank with a gun as a flood threatens. You may get a chance to try out some of the past—dancing to a bush band, tasting damper, pumping water, panning for gold or milking a cow. A ride in a gig helps one realise that even in the work-filled days of our forebears, there was enforced leisure time to meditate as they drove at a brisk twelve miles per hour into market.

For work manually they certainly did, in marked contrast to today when we pay for aerobic classes to keep us fit. They had to work hard in a pensionless world just to survive, and survival is a great incentive. It did not make them any better people than us; in many ways, we would consider them a callous crowd. Generally we have an ambivalent attitude, praising their endeavour and persistence on one day, and lambasting them on another for the problems of conservation we have inherited as they cleared and changed the land. In fact they were creatures of their time, some good, some bad, few saints or monsters, responding to their environment as best they could. They were people.

5 Trying out the flavour of the past at the Old Gippsland Pioneer Township: a dog-cart ride to the Sunny Creek school which was built in 1880 and is now re-erected at the site of the Township.

2

Land

There are two complementary ways of looking at land. One is a magic carpet approach, as if you could take to the sky and look down upon the area. From the air you can see the river, the mines, the pastures, the paddocks, the township with its industrial area, the forest, the mountain—and the whole can be spatially organised, neatly ordered into patterns. The organisation does not have to be topographical: you can equally take to the air and see your area divided into residential patterns—old township, postwar subdivision, market gardens. But it is the pattern you are concerned with—usually *general* statements about how the land is geographically ordered, or owned, or used, and how this changes, enabling you to theorise about what is happening to the people who live there. The other approach focuses on one *particular* piece of land in the whole. This is a view best taken with the feet substantially on the ground. The two are complementary because the general magic carpet view provides a context for the individual. The feet-on-the-ground view enhances the first by providing a tangible example of the prevailing order, or a timely reminder that prevailing orders are not immune to exceptions.

You may want to concentrate on one, but it is worthwhile to keep the other in mind. Researchers solely with their feet on the ground are unable to discern whether their particular concern is typical or not, and surely such knowledge would help provide some understanding of a particular situation. For example, if the selector of a piece of land can no longer pay the rent, then the knowledge that all his neighbours were having similar problems would lead you to ask why, and the answer may lie in the drought or bad crop prices of that year. Smaller patterns, however, may show that families that owned selections close together could cope better with unfavourable weather or prices and could pay their rents. Again why? Perhaps because they pooled their resources and could encourage some of their men to seek work elsewhere, such as timber-cutting, which would tide the families over the bad spell. Most amateur researchers are interested in a particular family and are essentially feet-on-the-ground people. If they do their research carefully and quote their sources exactly, their work provides another minute segment which goes into the pattern somebody else is weaving.

Patterns are important because they are the general statements of history. They enable us to compare and contrast and thus to bring order and coherence—understanding—to the many details and facets of the past. Nevertheless airborne viewers have the disadvantages of being so far away from the action that they are prone to conclude that 'down there' everybody is behaving and reacting in the same way. Life is too complex to warrant such assumptions, and bearing this in mind, this chapter turns first to land patterning and then comes to ground to take a closer look. We begin with the first inhabitants.

LOOKING AT PATTERNS

Aboriginal ownership

The land was supremely important to the Aboriginals. Families had particular rights to hunt in particular areas, and particular duties to look after the land. Norman Tindale has tried to map the lands belonging to different groups of Aboriginals across Australia. In 1974 he published a map, 'Tribal Boundaries in Aboriginal Australia', in conjunction with his book *Aboriginal Tribes of Australia*. Both are based on his extensive fieldwork stretching over more than 50 years as well as research into the ethnographic literature (the primary sources on the subject). However, to determine the boundaries of tribal land, it is necessary first to determine the question of what is a tribe. This has been much debated because it depends on sorting out the complex social relationships between Aboriginals, a task complicated by the fact that these relationships differed from area to area.

If you turn to anthropological literature to discover something about the original inhabitants of an area which interests you, you will meet a bewildering variety of terms used to describe Aboriginal social relationships. The family groups which generally lived, hunted and tended the land together—perhaps 30 men, women and children— are sometimes called 'bands' in the literature, and sometimes 'hordes', though this latter term has fallen from favour. Families also came together as 'clans'—to celebrate, trade and arrange marriages. More than anything else, clan membership and its associated religious emblem (or totem) defined whom one could or could not marry. Aboriginals identified themselves as members of a particular clan and also as members of a tribe. A tribe was a grouping of clans who intermarried and shared a common language, but tribal groups continually changed over time and space, as European nations have in the past. Individual Aboriginals identified themselves as people of a particular place, a particular family line, a particular totem, and a particular language group, but family ties often gave them rights and duties in areas quite distant from their own territory. Early white observers who noted the names of Aboriginal groups rarely distinguished between clans and tribes.

When it comes to discussing boundaries and the determining factors for these, again there is much discussion. The Aboriginals themselves were not given to pointing to precise marks, but they knew when they were in strange and forbidden territory, and resented and punished trespassing Aboriginal foreigners. Boundaries are generally considered to have been physiological ones, such as a gorge or mountain, or ecological, such as a change in vegetation, say from forest to heath, or where one predominant type of eucalypt gave way gradually to the predominance of another, box to ironbark perhaps. The more subtle transitions were imperceptible to the newly arrived Europeans and this makes it difficult to trust early white delineations of Aboriginal boundaries. Moreover, historians argue about the function of such boundaries. Tindale, for example, says that coastal dwellers did not claim the scarp of inland ranges, and maintained that some particular areas, such as mallee scrub or rainforest, required specialised skills if they were to be used efficiently. Other academics consider that areas were carefully divided to give different tribes approved access to a variety of foods, which meant crossing ecological lines to take advantage of seasonal diversity: prosperous was the tribe who could hunt the plains, fish a swamp and harvest a forest.

This variety of opinion makes matters complicated for the layman, but it is worth being aware that Aboriginal boundaries were not rigid lines on a map or marks drawn with a stick on the ground, but some sort of fluid arrangement, the subtlety of which the white man has yet to grasp. Perhaps the best one can indicate is that a particular Aboriginal group probably lived at or around the time of their first contact with Europeans in an approximate area. In the meantime the term 'tribe' will continue to be commonly used for a group of Aboriginals bound by economic and social ties.

A more fruitful way for the local historian to look at Aboriginal use of land may well be to concentrate on foci rather than on outer limits, to look at the places where it is known that Aboriginals gathered, places from which they moved in and out. A river could act as a central point, with a tribe having the right to gather food on both banks. This suggests the catchment area as the territorial range, and undermines the idea of a river as a 'natural boundary'. In fact, watercourses were occasionally dry, or at least shallow, and could often be forded at will. Rivers appear like boundaries on a map because they are drawn like a line, an easy way of demarcating territory for Europeans, but not for Aboriginals with a different mental image of the land. Geographic features were of some economic use or of religious significance or both. Whereas rivers were important for water and food, sandhills and rocks provided burial places and sacred sites; a waterhole could satisfy both demands. To such places, there was a strong and identifying emotional tie.

A large seasonal supply of food allowed tribes to meet for discussions and ceremonial gatherings including initiation rites, corroborees, and barter. An oft-quoted example is the Bogong moth 'festivals' held each summer on the peaks of the Snowy mountains. These tasty and nutritious moths were easy to gather, plentiful in the late spring and early summer, and attracted large numbers of Aboriginals each year. Of a similar nature were the Bunya Bunya nut assemblies in southern Queensland. These are two outstanding examples, but no doubt such occasions occurred on a smaller scale elsewhere and not simply between tribes but between the bands of one tribe.

Water and squatting

The availability of water is taken very much for granted these days, despite the efforts of the authorities to educate us on using it wisely. It is indeed a precious resource and in our dry continent has figured prominently in the lives of our predecessors. They have not generally treated it wisely either. This importance, this use and squandering of water, is an integral part of our history, and it repays the modern tap-oriented researcher to keep in mind the need for water as an important part of land patterns. The battle for water access, for example, was probably basic to Aboriginal–European conflict.

In contrast to the Aboriginals, the squatters, moving out with cattle or sheep into the country until they found and leased some watered land, established boundaries which they were quick to defend. The trouble is that, while the respective squatters often rode around the boundaries together and blazed the trees or ploughed furrows as markers, such signs no longer exist, and the written descriptions referring to such trees, in any case, are approximate in their estimates of distance and direction. Moreover, unscrupulous

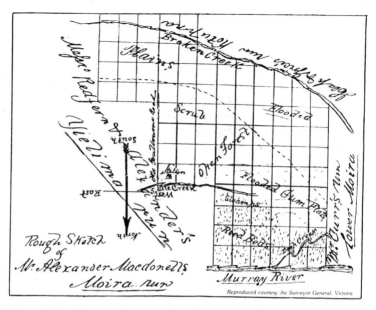

6   A map of the Upper Moira squatting run, covering what is now mainly the Barmah
Forest in Victoria. It comes from the file held by the Department of Crown Lands
and Survey in Victoria and was sent with the lease application requested by the
Government in 1847.

squatters were not above changing the line of an obliterated furrow in
order to enlarge·their domain. Some of the arguments which erupted
came before the Crown Lands Commissioner for a decision, and the
evidence of witnesses, still held in files on the disputed runs, makes
particularly fascinating reading and can throw light on the establishment of neighbouring stations (see p. 50).

These files may also contain hand-drawn maps of the pre-emptive
rights of the station showing buildings and yards. Pre-emptive rights
(shown as P.R. on maps) were the homestead sections of pastoral
runs bought by the 'pastoral tenant' (squatter) without having to
contest an auction, a privilege granted as some compensation for the
prospect of losing the run when the time came to sell it. (See
Victorian Government Gazette for 1851, p. 840 for the relevant
regulation.)

Some early maps show squatting leases, for example Ham's 1847
map of Victoria. There are also secondary sources which provide
similar information based on the best information the authors could
obtain but, like all secondary sources, subject to correction from
reliable primary sources together with your own detailed knowledge
of the local terrain.

Land sales and registration

The squatters leased the land from the government, or strictly speaking, the Crown through the government. Under English common law the ownership of all land in the realm is theoretically vested in the reigning sovereign. Thus all titles to Australian land issue from the Crown; it was this principle which was the undoing of John Batman's 'purchase' of land at Port Phillip from the Aboriginals. Until 1831 Crown land in Australia was mainly disposed of in grants, and afterwards mainly by sale. The Lands Department of the government managed the land if it was leased or occupied before it was granted or sold. It was responsible for surveying the land and then organising its sale.

Once the land was not vested in the Crown (or alienated as the expression is), it was of no further interest to the Department unless an allotment was bought back by the Department for a specific purpose. For example, the land on which the Necropolis at Springvale, Victoria, is sited was bought back by the Victorian Government in 1878. This 300-acre allotment had originally been the homestead block of a squatting run known as the No Good Damper station and was sold to the squatter Robert Robinson in 1853. The Department has no record of the sale of this section by Robinson to his brother George, or George's widow's sale of it to William Lempriere who then sold it back to the Crown for a cemetery. Such information is held in the Titles Office.

Parish maps and others

The Lands Department holds the cadastral plans. A cadastre is an official register of property, and cadastral maps or plans show the extent and ownership of land (for taxation) and the surveyed boundaries of Crown allotments, roads, townships and reserves. Each state is subdivided into counties which are then divided into parishes and townships, and further divided into sections and then allotments. Ask at your local shire or city office for the name of the parish of the land in which you are interested. The names have a history of their own, most often reflecting the names of the squatting runs or local Aboriginal place names in use when the parishes were set out. These maps are used by the Department for three specific purposes: first to mark Crown land reserved for some reason (foreshore, school, recreation, timber, etc.), second to show Crown land being held (not reserved), and third to show land alienated (sold) from the crown. If sold, the land is marked with the name of the first land buyer. (See pp. 58 and 60.)

It is essential to realise that a parish map does not present a static picture of the land at one particular time, except possibly the surveyed, pre-sale plan. It is a patchwork of information showing ownership at different times. As a parish plan or township plan became dilapidated from use or so worked over with changes that it was in danger of becoming illegible, it was replaced by a clean, new, redrawn plan and the old plan was 'put away'; the date when that occurred can be found from the date of the plan which succeeds it. The new plan, however, would not record current owners: it continued to reflect the three main concerns of the Department—Crown land reserved, Crown land held, and land sold to the first owners whose names is still carried. A series of 'put away' plans will show when land was reserved for specific purposes, when unreserved land was sold and to whom, and when alienated land was purchased by the Crown, perhaps for resale as in the case of soldier settlement, in which case the new owner or owners would have their name or names marked on the plan. In the example of the Springvale Cemetery, the first parish plan had 'R. Robinson' on the allotment, the later ones 'Transferred to her Majesty the Queen' (Queen Victoria) after it was bought back by the Crown, and then 'Necropolis Springvale' when the final decision was made to establish the cemetery. But subdivision of an allotment is not the concern of the Department and will not be marked on the parish map, nor will a change of ownership. 'Put away' plans are kept and can be seen if you ask—and pay.

Because Lands Departments are mainly concerned with survey, sale and management, their historical responsibility is less important. As queries have grown in the past few years, they have begun to organise themselves to cope with the demand for historical information; often, however, they charge for their help, so to minimise costs it is sensible to try other free sources first and to do your homework in order to know exactly what you want and to make the best use of the time for which you pay. Make a preliminary foray to see if they have any handouts. The Victorian Department, for example, issues an excellent booklet explaining what it holds, giving a short history of land legislation in that State and elucidating much of the notation which appears on maps. This Department advises writing before visiting the plans office and explaining what you want to see; this can reduce the time involved in research at the office, which is charged at a rate per hour.

Parish maps are the essential maps for the historian of land. They do not, of course, exist only at the Lands Department. Parish maps were freely sold and used for all sorts of purposes: they can be found in practically every collection of maps from the State libraries to that of your shire or city office. They turn up with all sorts of notations on them as other people use them for other reasons, and one place in which they sometimes surface is in government archival school files. These files record the early applications of parents for the establishment of a school. A map of the area marked with the proposed school site and the names and homes of the parents often accompanied the signed petition. Beside the family name was a notation of the number of children, for example, 1–3–2, which would indicate that there was one child of preschool age, three of primary-school age and two of secondary-school age in the family. As a basis for estimating the density of population such a map is a great help, although it is as well to remember that only the families with school-age children appear on the map, not the childless ones.

There are, of course, other maps: maps of rivers, road surveys, coastal surveys, of railways, of electric telegraph alignments, of sewers, all of which reside in different collections and various government department libraries. Maps of drains and floods would therefore be held by State river and water supply departments.

Estates and subdivisions

Land held by generations of one family or large estates with a few owners over some considerable time are not a problem to investigate because the past ownership is usually common knowledge locally and is simple to trace through rate books. Histories often feature these 'estates' because of their size and traditional aspect, but they are not necessarily important in the development of the district. The family or families may play a large part in the local government of the district or, on the other hand, they may hold aloof, respected but not participating in the local community. The land they hold, unless it is being used in some experimental way which provides a lead for neighbouring farmers, gardeners, orchardists, or vintners, does not change much through the decades and, for this tempting reason, attracts the historian, who breathes a sigh of relief at having 'done' that piece of history so easily.

But it is often the anonymous real estate agent or speculator from the nineteenth century who bought the land with the idea of subdividing and reselling who leaves a real mark on history. Not many settlers could afford to buy a Crown allotment of 200 or 300 acres at auction but some could buy five or ten or even 50 acres from a subdivision, and it was this sort of subdivision which brought people to an area to put up churches and start schools, while the big estates

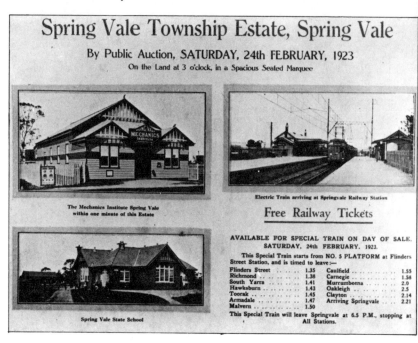

Spring Vale Township Estate, Spring Vale

By Public Auction, SATURDAY, 24th FEBRUARY, 1923
On the Land at 3 o'clock, in a Spacious Seated Marquee

The Mechanics Institute Spring Vale
within one minute of this Estate

Electric Train arriving at Springvale Railway Station

Free Railway Tickets

AVAILABLE FOR SPECIAL TRAIN ON DAY OF SALE.
SATURDAY, 24th FEBRUARY, 1923.

This Special Train starts from NO. 5 PLATFORM at Flinders Street Station, and is timed to leave:—

Flinders Street	1.35	Caulfield	1.55
Richmond	1.38	Carnegie	1.58
South Yarra	1.41	Murrumbeena	2.0
Hawksburn	1.43	Oakleigh	2.5
Toorak	1.45	Clayton	2.14
Armadale	1.47	Arriving Springvale	2.21
Malvern	1.50		

This Special Train will leave Springvale at 6.5 P.M., stopping at All Stations.

Spring Vale State School

7   Part of an auction poster, advertising a sale of land at Spring Vale, Melbourne, in 1923, which provides contemporary photographs of the mechanics' institute, school and railway station.

remained covered in scrub and cattle. It was the speculators who bought up paddocks on railway lines and surveyed through the reedy puddles a few tracks which they ornamented with grandiose names; and it was the real estate agents, who put out the posters, organised the free train rides and laid on the champagne or beer, who in fact christened many towns, laying out the streets and house blocks of today.

Subdivision and sale are normally the concern of the real estate agent. Land auctioneers' maps can be entertaining as well as useful provided you take the information with some scepticism. Essentially they are advertisements and they come with a sales pitch which varies from the brazen to the florid. A poster for the Gladstone Grange Estate near Dandenong in 1888 claimed the land as 'overlooking the site of the new Yarraman Park railway station'. If you had a telescope this was true, and the station itself was finally built in 1976! But these were the heady days of the land boom and speculators needed but faint excuse. Some nineteenth-century posters depict drawings of neighbouring prestigious houses, and in later years the agent would commission photographs of the nearby school, mechanics' institute, picture theatre or industry.

Although the auction day is prominently displayed, this rarely includes the year. To get that information you need some idea of the likely decade and a perpetual calendar (try an almanac or ask your librarian). This will tell you, for instance, in which year Wednesday, 29 September fell (1875, 1886, 1897). Do not forget to check the leap years which adds 1880 to this example. There is usually more than one date in a decade, but at least you have narrowed the field, and a check through the local newspaper around that date of each year, or a check of the rate book for the relevant years, should resolve the issue.

Tracing subdivisions and owners gets trickier as the land size gets smaller and as ownership changes. It is possible to do some tracing through the rate books but this depends somewhat on how clearly the shire secretary, or the clerk involved, identified the land being researched. He may just write Browns Road or he may use the parish Crown section number. A Crown allotment of over 100 acres is possible to track, but smaller township allotments are not usually numbered. The clerk generally put the names in alphabetical order and divided them into the electoral divisions of ridings (shire) or wards (city).

The Titles Office

The Titles Office is that part of the Registrar-General's department which records changes in land ownership. The Torrens system of land registration, designed to simplify the transfer of land, was taken up by all the Australian colonies (SA 1858, Queensland 1861, NSW, Victoria and Tasmania 1862, WA 1874). Under this system all land granted in fee (sold) was registered in a book and so were all subsequent owners, lessees and mortgagees. It is under this system that today's Certificate of Title recording the chain of land transactions is issued. These records can be 'searched', that is, looked at, but you need a certificate of title number, if possible, or at least a description of the land giving the parish, Crown allotment number, or lot and lodged plan number.

Before the introduction of the Torrens system it was not compulsory to register land although it was wise to do so under the Register of Common Law Deeds (or Old System), and a series of deeds was then required to prove ownership. (See *Australian Encyclopaedia* for further details.) The records under the Old System have been systematically traced back at one time or another, and the results, listing the changes in ownership, were set out in documents called search notes, which are now, of course, a valuable help to the historian. Not surprisingly, the State offices are reluctant to open their files for the perusal of amateurs. If you are absolutely stuck for some vital information, cultivate a friendly title searcher or pay one to do the work. If the task is not too complicated, it will be money well spent in saving hours of your time and effort elsewhere.

Twentieth-century maps

For research in the twentieth century two more types of map are useful. The first of these are army ordnance maps which are designed by the Royal Australian Survey Corps for the man on the ground so that they detail the vegetation and notable landmarks, even to houses and windmills in rural areas. World War I encouraged the Corps' expansion.

For other suburbs in which the growth has been mainly post–World War II, there are street directories. Your local or State library should hold a succession of these from which, if you have the patience, you can chart the extension of streets directory by directory as subdivisions flourished and paddocks disappeared. Old street directories are worth collecting, either for yourself or for your local historical society: they can be bought quite cheaply at opportunity shops or fairs if you keep an eye out for them.

There is no need to rely solely on other people's maps. Draw an outline of the district and photostat some copies. Your own historical atlas can record whatever you are interested in. For example, you could map contemporary references and sightings of birds and/or animals during an early decade, references to vegetation in primary sources over a certain period of time, the sites of Aboriginal camps and their known food resources within five to ten kilometres, squatting homesteads and run boundaries, patterns of first land buyers (settler, squatter, absentee owner, estate agent), use at different times (grazing, mining, market garden, residential, mining), the extent of floods in wet years, and so on. A good group project is to plot houses, stores, hotels, churches, etc. from the rate books. Take one year out of each decade and compare the difference. You can map land where settlers succeeded and where they left their blocks: that can bring to light some theories on success and failure.

---

8   The area now known as the City of Waverley, Victoria, with properties plotted from the Mulgrave rate book for 1864.

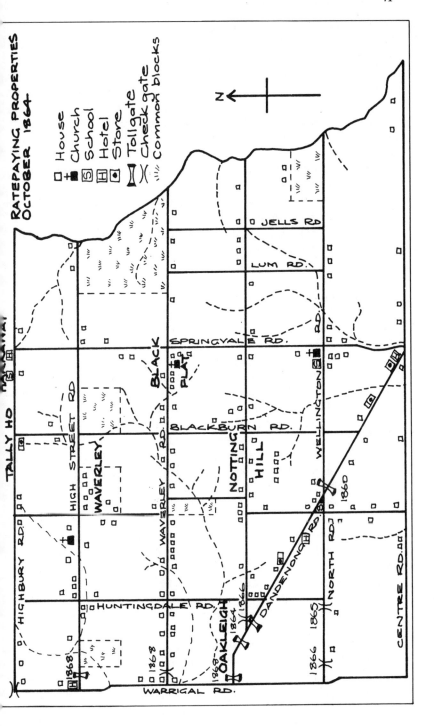

RATEPAYING PROPERTIES
OCTOBER 1864

☐ House
✝ Church
▩ School
Ⓗ Hotel
◉ Store
⧓ Tollgate
✕ Check gate
〰 Common blocks

N

TALLY HO

JELLS RD.

LUM RD.

SPRINGVALE RD.

BLACK FLAT

BLACKBURN RD.

NOTTING HILL

WELLINGTON RD.

HIGH STREET RD.

WAVERLEY

WAVERLEY RD.

HIGHBURY RD.

HUNTINGDALE RD.

OAKLEIGH

DANDENONG RD.

NORTH RD.

CENTRE RD.

WARRIGAL RD.

1868

1866

1864

1860

1865

1866

You can plot the residence of school pupils, which may lead you to the old citizens who know your area intimately. You should try to map the path of the original exploration, or perhaps the Cobb & Co. coaching route with its changing stations, now probably just coppices of trees. Maps made before and after the arrival of the railway throw up previously unconsidered hypotheses for thought and research. Or try to map ethnic groups from the census figures in the post-World War II period. It is amazing what the graphic representation of lots of details can add up to.

The National Library's publication *Australian Maps* aims to list all maps published each year in Australia and has been produced quarterly since 1973 with annual cumulations. All entries for 1961–73 have been gathered into one volume. The Library has an enormous collection of maps and also over half a million aerial photographs of Australia from the mid-century on.

Aerial photographs

Aerial photographs have been taken by the Division of National Mapping (NATMAP) since 1928 to help in topographic mapping. These photographs are taken systematically as the aircraft passes across the country in a 'run', the photographer aiming this camera through a hole in the underside of the aircraft directly at the ground below and taking photographs in a carefully regulated sequence to obtain a series of overlapping photographs in parallel strips. Since 1960 most of Australia has been covered in photographs on which one centimetre of the print represents 840 metres of land. Most photographs measure 23 × 23 cm and on this scale the side of a photograph represents about nineteen kilometres on the ground. Prints of almost all NATMAP air photographs can be ordered by mail. It is best to be able to give the correct reference number, but a clearly defined area, either sketched or designated with latitude and longitude, will bring results. NATMAP also holds the records of aerial photographs taken by other federal and State bodies and will tell you where these exist. The Australian Archives, for example, holds on microfilm the survey photographed by the RAAF over most of the coastline and the populated areas of Australia from 1930 to 1955.

There have been private aerial photographers operating since the 1920s, taking what are called oblique photographs (as opposed to vertical pictures) by handheld cameras pointed through an aircraft window. These photographs have been taken for a variety of reasons, from recording traffic to illustrating the site of a murder for a newspaper. All can help the twentieth-century researcher, especially the one whose subject is the growth of an outer suburb. Memories of this transformation from paddocks to patios are unreliable, particularly of the residents who have lived through it. More vivid are the memories of people who have lived in a particular district for a short period of time and have not moved back: they have a sharp mental picture of the place as it was when they were at school there, or worked there, or holidayed there, and can date it with some accuracy. Photographs, however, stop time, and can produce the contrast—the before-and-after illustrations. A larger gap in time is not necessary for a change in the landscape. Aerial photographs of around Hobart in the fiery summer of 1967 would show a dramatic difference. Flooding is another natural subject for aerial photography.

Many a misconception can be dispelled by aerial photographs. It is easy to deplore streets full of houses replacing hectares of eucalypts, haven for birds and wildlife. Early photographs may reveal the fallacy of that. In many cases, present suburbia contains more trees than the practically bare pastures which the subdividers bought, the bush having fallen last century to provide for the nearby city populations, so dependent on wood fires for heat and cooking. It is surprising that aerial photographs are not used more frequently as sources of information.

Now satellite photographs from Landsat offer an advance in valuable visual data. Landsat satellites are spacecraft of the United States National Aeronautics and Space Agency (NASA) which circle the earth every 103 minutes from an altitude of 900 kilometres. This means they can cover the earth every eighteen days and send back a picture covering an area 185 × 185 kilometres. The images returned to earth can identify forest, farm land, commercial areas, residential areas, lakes, rivers and oceans. It can also differentiate grain crops and legume crops, irrigated and non-irrigated crops, different sorts of timber, and so on. In Australia the images are received at Alice Springs and processed in Canberra. The colours in which the images are reproduced are not the normal ones of blue for the ocean and dark green for forest or those which an astronaut would see. In the Landsat images, deep water appears as black, vegetation as red, urban and industrial areas as light blue. For this reason, they take some adjusting to, but they give an unequalled opportunity to look at the patterning of a region, to see, for example, a metropolis in relation to the hinterland. The breadth of such views provides the ultimate so far in magic carpetography.

FEET ON THE GROUND

Professor A.L. Rowse's advice (*The Use of History,* 1948) to the historian to invest in a pair of stout walking shoes still holds good today. Walk or, at the very least, travel slowly around the district you plan to research. While man can change the course of rivers, and irrigate or drain, he has been less capable of moving mountains, despite an ability to lop difficult rises or quarry the sides of hills. It is precisely the contours which you need to note, partly because they are likely to be the same as those of a century or so ago, and partly because they do not appear on most maps, whereas the sea and rivers do. Actually being on the spot may answer questions, for example, why does the Princes Highway after kilometres of straight road bend when it reaches Dandenong instead of continuing straight on and over the Dandenong Creek? An ordinary map offers no clues. Feet on the ground will reveal that to continue the course of the road would have meant dipping into a depression and then climbing a small hill before the creek. In all likelihood, the first settlers found it easier to skirt a small swamp as well as the hill as they headed for what was probably a ford in the creek, a divergence the surveyor, Henry Boorn Foot, saw no reason to change. Viewing the terrain from a different angle also provides insights—the shore from the sea, the banks from the river. Even a train ride can show you an entirely different perspective from the one you get in a car, especially in the city when you see all those backyards.

In the past the terrain has largely determined a number of important issues—the place of settlement and the course of tracks, many now-busy freeways. Later it influenced the lines of drains and railways. An interesting exercise is to study the buildings on tops of hills, usually the province of the influential and rich. Was this a vestige of even earlier defence strategies, or a reflection of the view that low-lying air was unhealthy, or simply a desire to enjoy a view and look down on everybody else?

Geomorphology

Geomorphology (the science of land forms) is not really within the province of this book but we mention it here because it can explain why your part of the world is shaped as it is. The Murray, for instance, flows west generally except for the place where it suddenly turns south, and then, just after the Goulburn river joins it, west again. Why? At one stage the Murray evidently flowed continually west and parallel with the Goulburn until movement in the earth's crust thrust up land in its way, forcing the water to turn south along the front of the obstacle until it could commandeer the bed of the Goulburn. Knowledge of the Cadell tilt, as that raised land block is called, (after the red-headed river Captain who drove armadas of river pilots crazy by his method of snagging the river by cutting the logs just below the watersurface), makes sense of the river floods and flows in that region. In extensive floods it is said that the Goulburn waters force the Murray River to flow backwards past the face of the Cadell block and out the Edward River which is the Murray's northern escape route.

Geology

Geomorphologists are in close cahoots with geologists whose complex province is the earth's crust, the study of which reveals the history of the area going back over millions of years and gives the origin of existing topographic features. Unfortunately both sciences have a jargon of their own, and trying to understand the literature means finding a kind practitioner who will patiently explain what you need to know, or finding a secondary source which is not too complicated, such as a school text. Basic to understanding geology is the appreciation that the crust is viewed as layers, each named from the place in which it was originally identified or can be seen to best advantage. Thus the Red Bluff Sands formation in Melbourne can be seen in the valley of the Maribyrnong River and elsewhere but is named for its appearance at Red Bluff, Sandringham.

Second, geologists have arbitrary time divisions, commonly bandied about by the experts, but of little obvious relevance for most people, unless these dynasties can be translated into 'millions of years ago'. Even then the mind has difficulty in comprehending these vast dimensions, as geological time covers 4000 million years, of which Man has existed only for about the past million. A clichéd but enlightening exercise is to compress geological time into one year. In such a year the Quaternary period beginning one million years ago is less than the last day of the year, man appeared on the evening of that last day, and Captain Cook set sail for the Pacific one second before midnight.

Naturally the changes to the earth in the Tertiary and Quaternary times are the most important because they have been mainly responsible for the topography of today. The Miocene age was mainly cool, and in Pliocene time tropical rainforest extended down

Table 1   The division of geological time

Millions of 'Years Ago'	Eras	Periods
10 thousand	Quaternary	Recent/Holocene
1		Pleistocene
16	Tertiary	Pliocene
25		Miocene
40		Oligocene
65		Eocene
140	Mesozoic	Cretaceous
200		Jurassic
240		Triassic
290	Palaezoic	Permian
360		Carboniferous
410		Devonian
440		Silurian
500		Ordovician
570		Cambrian
	Pre-Cambrian	

to southern Victoria. During the Pleistocene period the earth experienced four major glacial periods or 'ice ages' in a period of repeated climatic changes. The effect in Australia is disputed, as is the climatic history of the last 10 000 years. One view is that the Pleistocene was followed here by a time of marked dryness, known as the 'Great Arid', probably between 8000 and 6000 years ago, but this is a hypothesis under attack. Geological knowledge keeps constantly moving forward, and the latest information needs to be sought in the most recent secondary sources rather than encyclopaedias.

A geological map is a plan of the distribution of the rocks in a given area as they are exposed at the earth's surface. Perhaps easier to understand is a geological cross-section which is the geologist's interpretation, based on surface geology and other geophysical data, of what you would find if you could take a deep slice of the earth between two surface points, like a slice of layered cake, and examine it. Some knowledge of the geological structure should help to account for the poverty or fertility of soil, the presence of springs, the level of the water table and the existence of natural resources such as gravel, gold or clay. Try your local State Department of Mines or its equivalent for their reports. Bores have probably been put down in your area at some time or other, even if it is only in the course of twentieth-century sewer construction. Many towns began as goldmining centres, and descriptions of the mines and mining can be found in the departmental reports, as well as the geological and mining journals of the last century.

Aboriginal occupation

Aboriginal occupation of this continent predates the white man's arrival by at least 40 000 years, but today there is likely to be little evidence of Aboriginal residence in your district. If you are lucky, the district may contain one of the few excavated camp sites of the many thousands which were occupied over the past 1000 years. The remains of such sites are only available in rock shelters and caves, in the shell middens mainly along the coast, earthen refuse and 'island' mounds around streams or lakes. Some burial grounds are known. Probably the commonest relic is the scarred tree where the Aboriginal has cut bark from a trunk for use as a shield, or a canoe, or for roofing. You can consult your local State archeological office to determine if any work has been done in the district. An intangible remainder may be the existence of Aboriginal names, some of which were commandeered by white men along with the sandhills, waterholes, creeks and landmarks to which they referred. Major Thomas Mitchell was one explorer eager to see that Aboriginal place names were retained. Beware, however, of Aboriginal names plucked from a name book because they sound picturesque.

Early descriptions

Having trudged around the terrain yourself, the next thing you want is somebody who has done the same thing several decades ago, and then written about it. The white explorer is your first hope; most kept journals for their contemporaries but were doubtless aware of the interest of posterity. Their explorations through an area are generally recognised and identified in secondary sources. You then have to chase up the existence of the journal, some of which are readily available as they have been published, and some of which only exist in manuscript form. Although the early explorers often quoted latitude and longitude, their field notes are not easy to interpret, even for professional geographers. Surveyors may be able to chart an exact course, as has been done with most of Major Mitchell's journey of 1836 into Australia Felix, the Western District of Victoria. Mitchell was the Surveyor-General of New South Wales and painstaking in his approach, yet he still made errors, and so it is not surprising that other explorers are less easy to trace. Charles Sturt's observations were infrequent and often wrong, while Hamilton Hume and William Hovell, arriving on the west coast of Port Phillip Bay in 1824, were convinced they had arrived at their planned destination of Westernport Bay. Nevertheless try to track your explorer if you can. If he left a map of some sort, so much the better. Just be aware that he, and you, may well not have it all quite right.

These journals of explorers are invaluable for their description of land which white men had never seen before. They are important because the ecology was very quickly affected by at least two changes. First the Aboriginals were discouraged from their regular practice of burning large areas of their territory, a practice which had produced grassy plains and open woodlands attractive to edible game. Second the white man introduced strange animals and new plants which, with deliberate destruction of the existing flora and fauna, drastically changed the existing patterns of vegetation. Not only did cattle and thrushes replace tiger cats and bustards but blackberries and willows managed to edge out kangaroo grass and wattles. The landscape looked different then. The swiftness of these changes is startling to document, but only the most perceptive of observers looking back over the same area appreciated that at the time. Keep this in mind even for descriptions made in the first decade of settlement.

Hot on the trails of the explorers came overlanders, botanists, squatters, surveyors, itinerant preachers, settlers of all kinds, many of whom were very minor explorers, 'the real discoverers of the Country' according to Governor Gipps. Their accounts and reminiscences, whether published or retrieved from an archive, take the most time to discover but the satisfaction is great. Reference is usually found in other secondary sources, perhaps just in a footnote, or on the walls or in the files of the local historical society. If you keep talking about what you are doing, you will find listeners responding with their own knowledge and leads to such information. Descriptions such as those by John Webster who overlanded from Sydney to Adelaide in 1840 provide the evidence for a reconstruction of the ecology. He kept a journal and later wrote of the country north of the Murray:

> We travelled leisurely now to allow horses and the cattle to feed on salt bush and the grasses which grow between. Salt bush does not exceed five or six feet in height. The leaves are bluish green, and are eagerly eaten by sheep, cattle and horses. They bear a small fruit or berry, that has a pronounced salt acid flavour ... What is the reason all the creeks are brackish here, indicating salt in the soil, and the number of sand hills we have seen, stretching from the mountainous country to Adelaide and perhaps further? Were the mountains islands at one time, and are we now travelling over an ancient sea bottom? Salt bush was succeeded by open forest parklike, with good grass and very large and high gum trees, through which emus and kangaroos scampered, and our dogs after them ... Flocks of parrots of gay plumage are everywhere, white and black cockatoos also.

J. Webster *Reminiscences of an Old Settler* p. 140

Notice too the perceptive questions, an irony when you consider our current problems with the salty watertable now killing pastures near the Murray.

Parliamentary Papers

In contrast to the difficulties of finding such accounts, the indexing of both the Parliamentary Debates and Parliamentary Papers makes them a fairly quick way to pick up local information. Some, such as the reports of departments responsible for building roads, may be illustrated with before-and-after photographs of the work being done. Others, such as those detailing proposed irrigation or concerned with mines, may contain maps. If you are lucky you may find a description like this of Norman Taylor, field geologist, exploring near the Genoa River in 1864. (Parl. Papers 1866, vol. 2, no. 14, p. 15).

> After this the track was very obscure, and we continually lost it—it traverses large rushy flats, with lagoons, for a mile and a half, then rises to an old deserted station, close by which are several diggers' holes, exposing a bed of drift pebbles, and boulders of all sizes. The ant-hills, of yellow clay and rotten wood, are very solid, and sometimes as much as six feet high. One horse lost ... The bed of the river is a perfect tropical jungle. ... Here I first saw a tree belonging to the laurel tribe ... called the 'Water-gum' ... The bark is silvery-white, the wood close-grained, and the column of it a faint yellowing grey—when polished it has a beautiful satiny lustre. Mr. Allen [a ship-builder] says it is the most useful wood he knows, as it readily takes any form when steamed—for shafts, wheel-spokes, handles of tools, etc. it is excellent. I also noticed a handsome tree bearing a great resemblance to the orange, having similar leaves and flowers, and a fruit or seed-pod of an orange-yellow colour, full of scarlet seeds, the rind of which tastes like the bitter orange. At night the air was full of the most discordant sounds ... made by owls, mopokes, and night-birds and animals of all sorts, assisted by frogs and the occasional howling of native dogs.

As settlement progresses, there is less description of the land, and more information on what is happening to it. When looking at the indexes keep likely subjects in mind, such as mining, water supply, irrigation, fishing, timber-getting, navigating rivers, collecting agricultural statistics, and establishing railways, as well as localities. Periodically many bodies presented reports to parliament and these were printed in the Parliamentary Papers for each session. There are also special reports from boards of inquiry and royal commissions; the most useful carry the minutes of the evidence in which one can get away from the bland, careful words of the bureaucrat and hear instead the voices of the witnesses—farmer, surveyor, fisherman, hotel-keeper, councillor—being questioned. Listen to William Lacey, a farmer at Drouin for about eleven years, speaking at the

Royal Commission on State Banking in the middle of the depression (Parl. Papers, 1894–95, vol. 3):

> 626.   Are you acquainted with the present condition of the agricultural interest?—Yes, practically I am. As far as I know, the farmers are in a very bad position; I do not know of a single good thing in connexion with them, or anything approaching a good thing. The district I come from is second to none in the colony for the quality of the land, and I am sure if the farmers did not do all the labour themselves they would not get a crust out of it. For instance, two years ago we were making between £6 and £7 per week by sending cream down to Melbourne; now we have the same number of cows and the same acreage of land, but the return is reduced to about £2 per week though just the same labour and capital are required to carry on the farm. As far as I can see all other things are reduced in proportion.

> 627.   What are your expenses in connexion with farming?—We have to work it with our own family; we do all the milking and so on ourselves except at harvest time, when of course we are bound to employ labour.

Parliamentary Debates are often most fruitfully examined under the name of the local member of parliament at that time. (See a handbook or biographical dictionary of politicians.) Most of his concerns, unless he was a prominent minister with a department, would be parochial. Generally when there was a change in the local government of his area, for instance, when a shire became a city, the member can be found on his feet, giving a potted version of the development and main features of the district concerned, so it may pay to check the index of the Debates, or *Hansard*, as they are now called, in the year or so before the official celebrations.

Land files

Individual voices speak also from the correspondence files of the Lands Department, now usually held in archives or being transferred to archives. These files were not concerned with sold allotments for which the Department no longer had a responsibility, but recorded the dealings of the Department with those people involved with reserved or leased land. Mention has already been made of the run files in which the squatters' disputes over boundaries sometimes appear (p. 34). The Department held these because the squatters had leases on their land for which they paid a rent.

In the days of the Selection Acts from 1861 to 1894 the land was leased until the selector had earned the right and paid the rent for a sufficient time to receive the freehold (ownership of the land). Such files provide the human side of the legislation, for here you will find the selectors' letters, usually to do with some problem or they would not be writing. (This is a matter of bias for the historian—good news receiving little publicity.) Most of the letters are unashamedly touching to read a century later, as they movingly speak of the tough times the writers are enduring and ask for extra time to pay the rent. Beyond the lack of punctuation and misspelling, they reflect pride, desperation, grovelling, defiance and self-pity, but generally the patient belief that the Department will recognise integrity and help an honest man in his plight.

The Department, usually understaffed and inadequately financed, made the selector wait for a reply. It had the unenviable task of sorting the genuine toiler from the hustler, reading between the lines as well as the words. The public servants' views can be discerned in the reports of the Crown land bailiffs and in the internal departmental memoranda written by officials without the faintest thought for posterity peering over their shoulders. And then the decision which can affect a family's life: 'selection to be forfeited' or 'more time allowed' scribbled on the back-turned corner of the page. Consider this letter:

> I beg to state that I am nine years on my land and during that time myself and my family have gone through great hardship and privations and two of my daughters have had to assist me on the land without shoes and we have had to live upon kangaroos and they have had to go out of sight when any strangers have come to the place being so badly clad. I have been thinking of selling out but I would like to try another year as I have been farming and carrying close upon thirty years and I am over fifty years of age. I feel loathe to part with my home as it is the first and if I lose it I fear it will be the last. I beg you will take my case under your favourable consideration.

It is nice to know that this man's descendants now live a moderately prosperous farming life on the same land. Fortunately, as rental conditions eased, the numbers of letters in the file decreased.

Disputes between neighbours are waged in the correspondence, and the fight of the squatter to hold the remnants of his run against the selectors can also be documented, all of which is very much grist to the social or local historian's mill.

Land files provide a fine example of the value of adding individual statistics together to form a generalised pattern. From a survey of several files, whether it is a sample or as many as exist, it is possible to derive a picture of the type of housing which was most common, and a simple description of the farms, including outbuildings, dams, fences, standing timber and crops (see p. 63). It is possible to plot on a map each selector's previous address and thus to discover the movement of families from one place to another. It is also possible to plot family-related settlement, although this information is supplied haphazardly. A comparison of applicants for a licence and applicants for the Crown grant some years later reveals the percentage who saw the whole process through, and those who for one reason or another left before they received their freehold. Even if this is done on a small scale for one area, it will enable that area to be compared with the success rate of selectors in a different part of Australia at the same time. Anybody planning to do such a general attack on a large number of files must be prepared to give it sufficient time and patience. A methodical approach, avoiding the backs of envelopes, is essential if you are extracting the same information from several files. A standardised form, worked out in advance and headed with space for the name of selector, parish, allotment number and size, file number and so on, with photocopies will save your time and sanity.

The clue to finding a land file is set out on the parish maps. Sometimes a land allotment will carry a fraction: the numerator or top number of the fraction is the serial number identifying the piece of land, and the denominator or bottom number indicates the section of the Land Act under which the allotment was alienated from the Crown (see p. 61). Others combine a letter of the alphabet with a number or numbers, with one number identifying the year and another a serial number given chronologically as each letter is received. For instance 89 would indicate 1889, and the figure 14832 would testify that the last letter had 14831 letters preceding it that year. The alphabetical letter identifies the subject matter or locality or sometimes the name of the enquirer. These latter files deal generally with matters unrelated to occupying land, like licences to extract gravel, grazing leases, the proclamation of townships and plans for reserves such as foreshores and water reserves. The system changed from time to time and your Lands Department may have a screed explaining all of this if you are lucky; if it does not, then you will have to ask or write, and perhaps that will help encourage the Department to issue some guidelines. File numbers for land selections and current Crown reserves will be found on parish and township plans, but other file numbers were generally recorded on working plans and not transferred to new plans. Most of the old, unused or 'dead' files have been transferred to State public record offices or archives and enquiries should be made there rather than at the Lands Department concerned. Even then finding a file number does not necessarily mean finding a file.

Local papers

The progress of farming life in the late nineteenth century can be documented from a close examination of local papers. Most people do not have enough time to work through every page, so reading the newspaper's report of the annual agricultural show, the most prestigious event of the farmers' year and held in the same week annually, may help. Occasionally competitions were held for the best local farm, and the winners' establishments were depicted down to the last harrow and pig. Or if the editor was short of material he might decide to run a series of articles on local farms, vineyards or industries, but you need to be lucky or conscientious to find these. If you do see such an article, check the weeks either side to find out if it is one of a series.

Gazetteers

Gazetteers were popular publications in the second half of the nineteenth century, the forerunners of today's street directories or tourist publications. They are geographical dictionaries giving a detailed description of a town. By comparing the entries in gazetteers published several years apart, you can detail the growth and development of an area. Similarly post office directories of addresses were used in a way comparable to the telephone directories of today. Bear in mind that, as with almost any publication, the information is already out of date by the time it is published, that is, another church may have been built in the time between writing the information and printing it, or the cordial factory may have closed. If you want exact dates, you need to go elsewhere for information, but at least these publications will give you a lead which helps to narrow the period requiring detailed research.

Field Naturalists' Clubs

Most of these sources refer to vegetation and animals with the general knowledge of the man of the time. The only observers who claimed some expertise and left records were the keen members of Field Naturalists' Clubs. Weekend excursions to the edge of the metropolis and a hike which took them from and back to the local railway station through the local scrub or forest were duly reported in their magazines. If you are dealing with what is now an outer suburb, you may find that these notes can provide at least some detail of the trees and flowers, perhaps birds, that they enjoyed seeing at the time.

Naming plants and animals

The names of Australian plants and animals can cause confusion. First, some names have changed over time. While we all know that the native bear is the koala, and a laughing jackass a kookaburra, how many people know that what was once called mutton fish we call abalone today, and what used to be referred to as tea-tree scrub was often swamp paperbark?

Second, the original common names differed from State to State. For instance, the tree now known as the alpine ash (*Eucalyptus gigantea*) was known as red ash and woolly butt in Victoria, gum-top stringbark and white-top stringy bark in Tasmania, and Australian oak, Tasmanian oak and Victorian oak in New South Wales.

Third, the constant harking back to familiar names and plants means that Australian trees and plants were often given English names although they bore no botanical relationship, hence the oaks, cedars, pines, ash, box, beech and other such names. 'Wattle' was applied to any tree whose branches were sufficiently pliable for weaving in the rough wickerwork which formed the basis for wattle-and-daub houses.

It is only since the 1940s that an attempt has been made to standardise the names of Australia's commercial trees, fishes and plants. Names still vary tremendously. The white-faced heron (*Ardeanovae hollandiae*), Australia's most common heron, is best known as the blue crane.

If a plant, animal or bird is described, you may be able to identify it by reference to a current natural-history reference book. This is not as easy as it sounds. To some degree it depends on the detail and accuracy of the original description. Charles Sturt, on a droving expedition along the Murray, wrote of seeing '[Aboriginal] burial places in every sand hill, three of which contained upwards of fifty graves, perforated in every direction by rats'. 'Rats' probably refers to the rabbit bandicoot or bilby, which do not inhabit the area now. Five years later in the same place Edward Curr wrote of 'bellbirds, their silvery notes . . . always ringing'. From checking a recent book on Australian birds that could be perhaps the bell miner (*Manorina melanophrys*) or the crested bellbird (*Oreoica gutturalis*). It really needs an expert to work that one out. Curr also describes 'clumps of reeds (along the Murray) up which climbed convolvulus in waste luxuriance . . . opening a hundred azure chalices to the south wind'. Probably a botanist could identify the convolvulus but it is difficult to find a blue-flowered climbing plant to fit that description in a quick flit through some books on Victoria's native plants.

To make it clear which animal, bird or plant you mean (apart from the perfectly well-known ones) it may be as well as to include the Latin names (in italics), or if that destroys the feel of the text, to include the vernacular or common name in the text and elucidate this with the Latin name in a footnote. The Grey-crowned Babbler is also commonly known as the Cackler, Chatterer, Catbird, or Apostle bird, while early bushmen referred to it as the Mocking bird. Its scientific name is *Pomatostomus temporalis*. Incidentally, while a kangaroo is a kangaroo, there are different kinds, and if you can identify the appropriate sort so much the better.

Lastly, it should not be assumed that because native plants or birds or animals live in a particular area now that they have always done so. Some native vegetation has spread in the ecological changes effected by white settlement, for instance, coastal tea-tree (*Leptospermum laerigatum*) on the Mornington Peninsula in Victoria is now much more prevalent than it was formerly, thanks to the destruction of the open woodland of Drooping Sheoak (*Casuarina stricta*) for the ovens of Melbourne. Similarly white ibis (*Threskiornis molucca*) breed on the Mornington Peninsula, but primary sources make plain that this did not occur earlier, and seals frolic around man-made marine structures in Bass Strait which did not exist before 1970. Koalas now happily munching on eucalypts by courtesy of the State's Wild Life Department do not constitute proof that they did so, in that particular place, a century or so ago.

A CASE STUDY IN LAND USE: MORDIALLOC

To follow how this all works in practice, let us take a piece of land and so some short-term and long-term research on its use. The place where a watercourse meets the sea seems to make for an interesting conjunction, to judge from the number of cities on such sites, offering a variety of possibilities.

The terrain

Mordialloc is a suburb 27.5 kilometres from the heart of Melbourne on the east coast of Port Phillip Bay. It differs from other bayside suburbs in that it bestrides a creek which empties into the sea. North of the creek on a small hill is the township—shops, post office and station, with churches and school on the other side of the line. On a Saturday morning, it is busy with shoppers and patient boys with bicycles waiting to cross the very busy Nepean Highway which bisects the shopping centre. Puttering around on the creek and along the beach there are people 'messing about in boats', and the red sails of the Mirror dinghies flick over the waves. There are no cliffs and you can see the beach stretch away to the south, and the pier jutting out to the north side of the creek's mouth. The houses ride the side of small undulations, rather delapidated weatherboards closer to the centre and the sea, tending to younger versions in brick further away. After a pleasant sunny tour, it seems almost a shame to retire to the quiet, dim recesses of the La Trobe Library at the Melbourne State Library, but here we hope, enlightenment of a different kind awaits us.

The *Concise Oxford Dictionary of English Place Names* does not list Mordialloc, so it evidently has not been named by some nostalgic early settler. *Place Names of Victoria* (L. Blake, Rigby, 1977) suggests that it is Aboriginal for 'near little sea' (Moody or Mordy Yallock). However there is no tangible evidence of an Aboriginal presence in Mordialloc today and the Victoria Archaeological Survey has no excavations or sites marked in the area.

Mordialloc was part of the Moorabbin Road District set up in 1862 which became the Moorabbin Shire in 1870. In 1920 it was part of the Borough of Mentone and Mordialloc severed from the Shire. This was changed by proclamation to the Town of Mordialloc in 1923 and to the City of Mordialloc in 1926 (Municipal Directories).

La Trobe Library maps

On the first floor of the library 107 heavy tomes of a large collection of Victorian Lands Department Survey maps offer all sorts of dusty possibilities. The index gives the numbers of the parish and township maps of Mordialloc and we lug the first volume to a table.

The first parish map reproduced here (part only) is unusual in that it shows the vegetation and waterholes which many such maps do not. The allotments have been numbered and the acres, roods and perches appear on each. (There are 4 roods in 1 acre and forty perches in 1 rood). But there are no names apart from Macdonald near the coast and no houses except a homestead near the creek and its bridge. Another usual feature are the tracks shown between the existing towns. Part of the parish is marked Reserve, which may or may not indicate a place for a township. There is no indication otherwise that a town is planned. It is dated 9 May 1855. A likely supposition is that this is the first surveyor's map of the parish before the land was sold because no names appear on any of the allotments. This parish map is that of the parish of Mordialloc, and the creek is part of its southern boundary, so another parish map will need to be looked at south of the creek—that of the parish of Lyndhurst.

In the same volume is another map dated 13 June 1863. It shows a township laid out at least between McDonald Street (that name

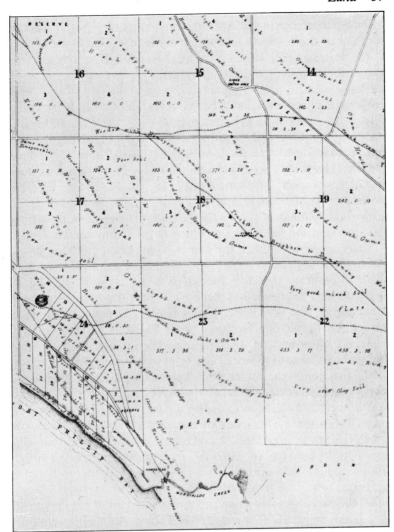

9   Portion of the Parish of Mordialloc from a map dated 9 May 1855. Map Collection, La Trobe Library, State Library of Victoria.

again) and Warren Street (known today as White Street). The area previously marked Macdonald is now marked Pre-emptive Right (see p. 34 for an explanation). The squatter usually bought the land around his homestead which was sited in the best spot close to water. In this case, if that was his homestead on the first map, Macdonald has not included it, but there is a hotel on the P.R. now marked as the Mordialloc Hotel (still there). The other interesting point on the map is that the township subdivision makes no allowance for the 'aboriginal graves' marked on it, suggesting that possibly Mordialloc was a site of some importance to the Aboriginals and that their burial grounds were not of much importance to the white man.

The next map reproduced is dated 12 August 1877 and is a sketch map of the township, and the information it provides you can work out for yourself.

The next relevant map is dated five years later (1882). It shows the railway line, which the previous map did not. It at least links A. Macdonald and the P.R. together so you can fairly safely theorise that A. Macdonald was the local squatter at the time of the land auctions. His name also appears on allotment 22, section 1, as does that of J.S. Parker for allotments 17, 18, 19, 20, 21 and 22. This means that A. Macdonald and J.S. Parker bought this land from the Crown and their names stay on the parish map unless the Crown buys back the land for some reason. When did they buy the land?

There are no dates with the names. Quite often there are dates, which is useful because a date *may* be that of the Crown auction. More often it is the date on which some clerk in the Lands Department completed and signed the title deed to the Crown allotment. Before 1862 it was not compulsory to register land deals but sensible to submit a Memorial of the Exchange to the Registrar-General's office and, in time, most people did just that. At least that gives you a date to work back from in the government gazette, should that periodical's index prove to be unhelpful. So a date of any sort is a blessing because otherwise we have to search for it. The land is very likely to have been sold after the first survey and our earliest map is May 1855. The index of the 1855 *Government Gazette* is unhelpful, not listing Mordialloc in its index for that year, but with beginners' luck we find (p. 1109) these allotments up for sale a month later on 5 June 1855. This is not a very satisfactory way to look for land sales or township allotment sales. Sometimes they are indexed under the parish or town name and sometimes a list of sales is kept in your Lands Department or public record office. Another possibility is the index to the local newspaper, if it exists, because the sale would have been advertised.

There are two other points of interest on this 1882 map. The first is that the public park and the recreation reserve both have their gazettal number. The park is gazetted as 73/1962 which means the 1873 *Government Gazette*, p. 1962, and the recreation reserve as 76/339 indicating page 339 in the 1876 *Gazette*. These pages will give an exact description of the area set aside.

---

10   Sketch map of the township of Mordialloc, dated 12 August 1877. Map Collection, La Trobe Library, State Library of Victoria.

L.5294

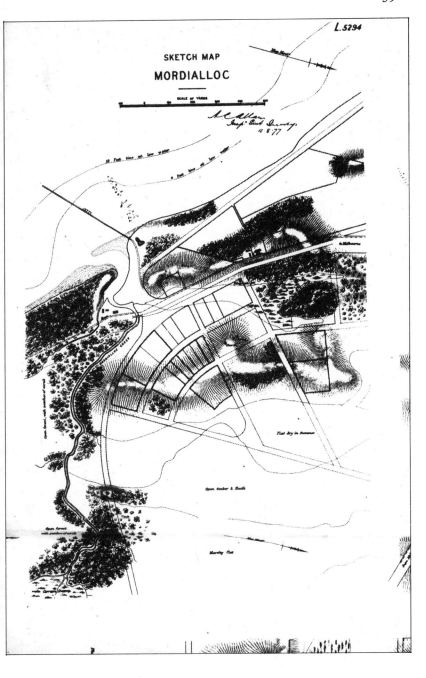

60

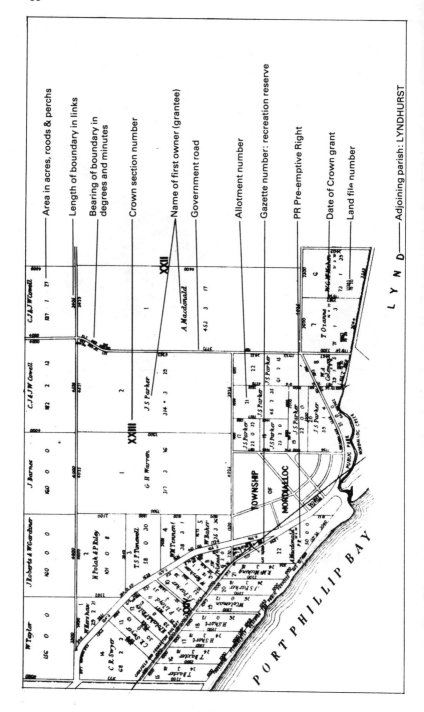

Area in acres, roods & perchs

Length of boundary in links

Bearing of boundary in degrees and minutes

Crown section number

Name of first owner (grantee)

Government road

Allotment number

Gazette number: recreation reserve

PR Pre-emptive Right

Date of Crown grant

Land file number

L Y N D —— Adjoining parish: LYNDHURST

The second point is that three blocks are marked with a fraction, the common denominator being 1920. This is a reference to a land file. The top number refers to the individual's file, the bottom one to the Land Act concerned.

Similar numbers cover the parish map to the south of Mordialloc— the parish of Lyndhurst. So the land was evidently taken up under the same Land Act—which we need to identify. The booklet from the Lands Department will reveal that 1920 identifies the relevant Act as the Victorian 1869 Act, and the *Australian Encyclopaedia* gives the background to these 'Selection Acts' but not in sufficient detail. We can try the secondary source listed in the *Encyclopaedia's* bibliography or go straight to the Act at a university law library.

The 1869 Act aimed to help small farmers take up land. Clauses 19 and 20 refer to the licence and leasing provisions. Approved applicants for an allotment were given a provisional licence for three years. During that time they paid rent of two shillings per acre a year and were expected to live on the allotment, cultivate one acre out of every ten, to fence it and to effect improvements (outbuildings, dam, clearing, etc.) to the value of twenty shillings per acre. If they did this they could get a lease for the next seven years and go on paying the two shillings rent, or immediately pay off the balance of fourteen shillings per acre, and receive the Crown grant so that they owned the land.

So one can generalise that the land south of Mordialloc was selected some time after 1869, and questions immediately come to mind? What crops did they grow? Was it easy to pay the rent? Where did the selectors come from? Were they poor or well established financially? There is an opportunity here to take out some statistics on the selectors and to look at general patterns.

But that is all homework and thought between one morning's profitable work at the La Trobe Library and a decision to come down to earth for a look at some individual files on the next excursion.

Public Record Office files

So to the Public Record Office in Cherry Lane, a misnomer if ever there was one in the thistle- and factory-ridden paddocks of Laverton North. The Office requires researchers to sign in/out and to sign for files. The records are divided into series, subdivided into units. Each series is numbered in an index. The series number also leads to a

---

11   Portion of the Parish of Mordialloc, Victoria, from a map dated 1882. Map Collection, La Trobe Library, State Library of Victoria.

descriptive record of what documents are held under that series, although the description varies from a detailed listing of every record in each unit to an uninformative sentence or two on the records included. In the index the VPRS (Vic. Public Record Series) number for the land files sought is 625, and in another index the original individual file number (top number of the fraction) leads to the Unit number. Nine files are of interest—those of Coleman, Ozanne, and McMahen in the Parish of Mordialloc, and McCaffrey, Rawlings, McSwain, H. Brown, and Owens in the Parish of Lyndhurst immediately to the south of Mordialloc. These particular files were numbered alphabetically under the first letter only of the surname as people were licensed to take up the land (a process called selection and the licencees, selectors). So the Browns apparently applied together as they both have successive numbers, 10298 and 10299, suggesting that they went along together and are probably related. Their records are in the same box, as are those of Ozanne and Owens in another, but Ozanne's number is 18867, whereas Owens is 18889, which indicates that Owens applied later than Ozanne. (In the country the selector applied at the nearest Land Board so it is necessary to work out at which town the Board sat. Neighbouring parishes could attend differing Boards, which is confusing. Some registers to these country files still exist.)

Each file starts at the back, as the clerk put each new piece of information into the file as it arrived without disturbing the rest, so the last piece of paper in time is therefore the first in the file. These files begin with the Crown grant on top and move back in time to the application for a licence. So we begin at the back.

The files, particularly the lease applications with details of fencing, crops, housing and improvements, provide much information. From a magic carpet point of view, the overall picture is that the land near Mordialloc is so wet that the selectors cannot live or grow crops successfully on their selections. It is also apparent that some drainage scheme is afoot during the early part of the seventies for which the selectors pay an annual rate. Perhaps the drainage scheme is why, despite the wet terrain, they have all persisted in acquiring their Crown grants (that is, have paid for and own the land) by 1881 except the original selector of Rawlings' allotment who turns out to have been Donald McSwain. That is a proposition to bear in mind, but far from proved because the Act's regulations require residence and cultivation in the licence period, which it is quite apparent has not occurred; indeed Norman McSwain asserts in a letter in his file that it is 'utterly impossible to comply with the conditions of the licence'.

On an individual level, the files reveal much personal information about the selectors. William Coleman is the son of the owner of the

Bridge Hotel at Mordialloc, McMahen a market gardener who lives with his father one and a half miles away, Robert is Hugh Brown's son, the McSwains are brothers, and Ozanne comes from Guernsey, one of the Channel Islands. The file of Owens is particularly helpful on Mordialloc and his lease is reproduced here. It shows him to be the local storekeeper.

Three of the files have personal letters to the Lands Department in them. Norman McSwain is particularly graphic in describing the local conditions, mentioning the drain extending the creek, the lack of roads, and the new (c. 1876) bridge built over the drain, (not the main bridge and presumably the forerunner of the existing Wells Road bridge). The first page of a letter in Ozanne's file is reproduced.

In Hugh Brown's file is pinned a full-scale map entitled *Plan and Sections of the low land comprising the Carrum Swamp* dated 25 August 1871. Here is Mordialloc with its township plan, and directly south of the creek the parish of Lyndhurst showing the entire swamp with its watercourses, sandy flats, sand ridges and areas of scrub marked on it as well as the allotments. It would appear to be the first map of that part of the parish of Lyndhurst, showing vegetation and surveyed allotments but no names. The files showed that the earliest selector was there on 1 September 1871 and possibly this was when selection of the swamp was first allowed. A check of the 1871 *Government Gazette* (p. 1388) confirms that proposition. It is now possible to describe accurately the swamp in 1871—quite a find.

On the whole the selectors we have looked at are mainly locals and either men with money or the sons of comfortably-off families. The exception is Ozanne, who gives his address as Western Dining Rooms, William Street, Melbourne, and his occupation as labourer. They appear to have emigrated from Britain, Ireland and Scotland. This is, however, a small sample of the total number of selectors who appear on the map of Lyndhurst, and to come to some general conclusions about the group, we would need to look at the other files also. We have done enough for one day.

Nevertheless we still want to find out about A. Macdonald, so back again for another day. The Record Office has the run files (now also on microfiche), and the Series (VPRS 5360) index lists Mordialloc as the name of the run. The file shows letters from Alexander Macdonald (and here is his signature, so it is worth noting how the man spells his name). The letters are concerned with his efforts from

12a/b (*Overleaf*) The application for a lease of his selection by Robert Owens p. 2 shows details of the fencing and improvements he had made in the previous three years; page 3 shows details of his residence, occupation and other property. Reproduced by permission of the Keeper of Public Records, Victoria.

Further Particulars to be furnish... Licensee when making application for Crown Grant or Lease und... ...tion 30, Land Act 1869.

Fencing :—	Description thereof.	No. of Chains.	Cost per Chain.	Total Cost.		
				£	s.	d.
	Post and 3-rail, split stuff ...					
	Post and 2-rail, ~~and~~ 1 wire.	12/-	15/-	9	-	-
	Post, 1 rail, and 2 wires	52-72 lds	14/-	36	18	-
	Post and wire					
	Stone wall					
	Stub, or picket					
	Log					
	Chock and log					
	Log and brush					
	Brush					
	Have you arranged with occupiers of adjoining lands for payment of any portion of the above fences ?	No				
	Who are the occupiers of the adjoining lands ?	Hugh Brown North R. Byrne South, R. Owens S.E. and Swamp drain on E.				

• Cultivation :—	Number of Acres Ploughed and Cultivated.	Cost per Acre.	Nature of Crop.	Yield per Acre.		
	First year too wet to cultivate					
	Second year Ploughed 7 ac.	£2..	Lucerne & turnips	14	-	-
	Third year 7 ..	£3..	1½ ac mangolds not yet			
	Ploughed 2 more		4 ac turnips 2 aca mataya	21	-	-

Buildings :—	Description.	Dimensions.	Materials.			
	2 Roomed cottage	22 + 10 by 9ft	Weatherboard & Hardwood & bricks	36	-	-

Water Storage:—	Description.	Dimensions, &c.				
	Dam					
	Reservoir					
	Well					

All other Improvements :—	Particulars of Nature and Cost.					
	Contribution to General drainage		5	6	-
	29 Chains of drain	6/-	8	14	-
	17 do do + bank	4/-	3	8	-
	10 do do	4/-	2	-	-
	8 do do	4/-	1	-	-
	14 do do	3/-	2	2	-
	Total Cost of Improvements ... ... £		139	3	-

		Further Particulars—continued.
ation for Crown Gra		
Total Cost.	...any rooms does your dwelling-house...?	Fifteen Rooms beside various out-buildings.
	...permanently attached to the soil of this ...ement?	No. It is one mile distant
	...you resided here continuously?	Yes for the Past 18 years.
	...you any other place of abode? If so, ...here?	No other place of abode.
	...here does your family reside?	In Mordialloc
	Have you or do you follow any other, if so, what business or employment?	General Storekeeper & Lodging House Keeper
	Do you own any land in fee-simple? If so, state the number of acres, situation, and purpose to which it has been applied	about 79 acres in Mordialloc 73 acres of which has been recently purchased the remainder is under cultivation of a general kind
	Do you hold any land under another license or lease from the Crown? If so, state the number of acres, situation, and purpose to which it has been applied	No I do not
	If in either of the above two last-mentioned cases the land has been cultivated, state the particulars thereof as fully as hereinbefore required, and also the distance in each case from this allotment	The Land above alluded to is distant about one mile from the selection
	If the condition of residence has not been complied with, state the reason why not	Because I and my family have continuously resided in Mordialloc distant one mile from the selection.
	If the condition of cultivation has not been complied with, state the reason why not	On account of the land being under water
	If the land is not enclosed as per licensed boundaries, state the reason why not	Because it was partly under water & a large drain was being constructed at the end of my selection by the Dandenong Road Board

Signature— Robert Owens

Occupation— Store Keeper

Address— Mordialloc

Declared upon oath at Cheltenham in the Colony
of Victoria, this 28th day of August
1876, before me, one of Her Majesty's Justices of the
Peace in the said Colony.

James Jamison J.P.

* This was read over to the declarant, in my presence, this   day of   187 .

J.P.

Mordialloc October 8/ 1874

Mr Commissioner of Crown Lands
                    Melbourne

                Sir

                    In making application for
a lease of Allotment 7 Cabreen Swamp I
have the honor to explain the reasons for
the omission of Claws 3 & 4 from my declaration
as licensee

In the 1st year of the License I got post ready
to fence the ground but could not erect
any owing to the ground being covered with
water

In the 2nd year I put up 24 chains of post
nearly one third in water but could not
erect any more from the water becoming too
deep

In the 3rd year I managed to complete much
of the fence carrying the post where the ground
would not sustain a cart

In the later part of February last the only
time that the allotment as been nearly dry &
since I selected I engaged a plowman to till
10 acres but before he could begin the ground
was again covered with water

I have paid 4/ per acre per year towards the
drainage of the Swamp which was begun
in 1872 but only 20c of the Main Drain
then cut last Summer a further lenght was
cut past my land but the water was not
drained from it The water which flood my
selection came from the west of Cheltenham
and to remove it I am under obligation

February 1852 to buy some of his squatting run and particularly to include four or five acres on the creek where he has two cottages, a kitchen and a stockyard. It appears that in 1851 the Guardian of Aborigines, William Thomas, had applied for the land to be allocated as a reserve for the Aboriginals and this included Macdonald's homestead. On 28 December 1852 Macdonald writes that he has been a squatter for eight years at Mordialloc, in May 1854 for nine years. If correct, that would suggest that he came into the district between June and November 1844. In 1854 he says he has a large, young family! He carefully draws a map on one letter to illustrate the situation. The issue is not resolved on the file—presumably the papers are missing. It would seem Alexander lost the battle, for, to judge from the maps we saw earlier, he decided evidently to make a profit from necessity and build a hotel on the brow of the hill as the creekside was no longer available.

Browsing through indexes is a good habit for the historical researcher and checking on 'Aborigines' suggests a series which is described in detail. (VPRS 2896, Registered Inward Correspondence to the Surveyor-General, Board of Land and Works and Board of Land and Survey relating to Aboriginal Affairs.) A skim through the record of the series produces pure gold. First a memorial (a written representation to the authorities) from the people of Mordialloc, dated 8 March 1858, to sell portion of the Aboriginals' reserve at Moody Yallock for a township, signed by several Chinese. It says the creek is an important fishing and salting station which employs over 100 people who have nowhere to build houses and live in 'comfortless tents on the creek'. The Aboriginals, the memorialists maintain, seldom visit, and then only one or two. William Thomas's opinion, sought by the Board of Land and Works, disputes this, describing Mordialloc as 'a casual fishing spot for the last nineteen years' and 'the Chinese are the salters, in fact the principal inhabitants'. They have encroached on the reserve but get on better with the Aboriginals than the whites. Thomas asserts there are ten or more local Aborigines left and other tribes visit 'Moody Yallock'.

Thomas, of course, must be checked out in the *Australian Dictionary of Biography* (vol. 2, p. 518). He should know what he is talking about as he has been assistant protector for the Aboriginals in the Westernport region since 1839 (the nineteen years mentioned above) and has travelled extensively around the area with them. Naturally

---

13 The first page of a letter from the file of Thomas Ozanne. It is typical of letters to be found in the land files in that it sets out to explain why he has been unable to fulfil the provisions of the Act under which he selected his land allotment. Reproduced by permission of the Keeper of Public Records, Victoria.

Jos. Procter   Mordialloc
James Coleman   do
Alfred Coleman   do
Henry Gomm   Morabbin
George Gomm   Morabbin
J.A. Thomas   Mordialloc
Campbell Peter   Mordialloc
Comre Series   do
Mc Veagh   do
R.H. Harris   Mordialloc
Joseph Ween   Mordialloc
John Cartmell   Mordialloc
James Devenport   Mordialloc
John Ween   do
Thomas Barroughs   do
John Williams   do

廣東香山順咸魚寮   萬地了吵唐人
雷來有   萬地了吵唐人
程進財   萬地了明唐人
盧亞信   萬地了吵唐人
黃亞生   萬地了吵唐人
翠潤綉   萬地了卯唐人
                               萬地了吵唐人
雷實愿丁   萬地吻吵唐人
孫阿朝   萬地吻吵唐人
鮑阿文   萬地丙吵唐人

his occupation and his action in obtaining the reserve for the Aboriginals means that his sympathies lie with them. His papers, according to the bibliography, are at the Mitchell Library in Sydney. Thomas will have to wait.

For we are not yet finished at the Public Record Office. Two years later, over the summer of 1860–61, Thomas is protesting against the appropriation of the Aboriginal land for a Farmers Common (unfenced and unused land set aside for grazing by a community of people). It is clear from the correspondence that it is, in fact, being used for that purpose; Thomas writes of the grass being uprooted by pigs belonging to the occupier of the neighbouring inn (Macdonald?). But Thomas is fighting a losing battle—the Mordialloc Farmers' Common is declared (check the 1861 *Government Gazette*, p. 380— February, 4960 acres, a month later extended by 3000 acres and Moorabbin added to the name). Moreover, this issue brings the question of a township back into official consideration. Writes the Assistant Commissioner of Lands and Survey:

> the existence of an Inn close to the Mordialloc Creek and the location on the reserve of a numerous population of fishermen and holders of tent-permits render the reserve peculiarly unsuited for a place of resort for Aborigines. I think it would be expedient to establish a village on this reserve and set apart for the Aborigines an equivalent portion of land in a less objectionable locality.

The 'equivalent portion' which he had in mind was probably the strip of land between the beach and the Carrum Swamp which he considered was 'not likely to be sold'! A township does not seem to have been gazetted but streets are laid out by 1863, as we already know. So lucky Macdonald has ended up with 50 acres and a hotel adjacent to a township subdivision!

We should not neglect two other recommended lines of enquiry before leaving the Public Record Office—schools and rate books. There are no maps, as it turns out, in the file on the Mordialloc State School (VPRS 795) at the Public Record Office, but it has some written description. The first application for a school is made on 8 February 1865 for allotment 3, Section VII, township of Mordialloc. A.B. Orlebar, the Schools Inspector, reported in September of that year that there were 'about 20 houses in the township but the greatest part of the population live towards Dandenong'. He describes the townsfolk as fishermen and woodcutters, those further inland as small

---

14 The signatures on the memorial requesting the establishment of a township at Mordialloc. Such documents help to establish who was where when. Reproduced by permission of the Keeper of Public Records, Victoria.

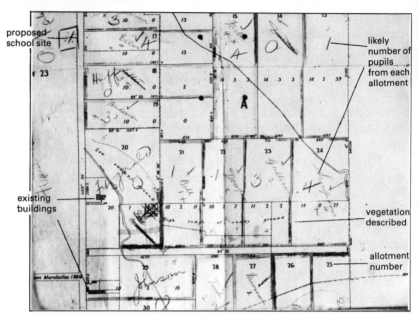

proposed school site

likely number of pupils from each allotment

existing buildings

vegetation described

allotment number

15   Part of the Small Holdings near Mordialloc map found in the Braeside school file, useful because it shows the existing buildings and vegetation as well the names of settlers written on to it. Reproduced by permission of the Keeper of Public Records, Victoria.

farmers or graziers—'they were generally poor'. Not much in words, but a very valuable description from an observer with no axe to grind who has gone to Mordialloc specifically to observe and report in an objective way to the authorities. He makes no mention of any Chinese.

There is a wealth of incidental information with a list of the inhabitants and children in the Application for Aid to New Schools dated 24 March 1865. Here is Alexander Vause Macdonald with a son named after him, aged twelve, and a daughter, Caroline, aged six.

The other nearest school is Braeside, just outside our area of research. It begins much later—in 1915—but there are some years of correspondence in the file before that, the school being called at first the Mordialloc Settlement School. There is considerable discussion about whether the 'settlement' is a viable project, and eventually a map appears headed Allotments for Small Holdings near Mordialloc and it is clear that the 453 acres Macdonald had purchased east of Mordialloc (allotment 22, section 1) has been bought back by the Crown and carved into 38 allotments ranging from nine to fourteen acres in size on which has been settled some farmers as market gardeners, poultry-farmers and so on. The reproduced portion shows the sort of detail available. It details one of the two houses on the block, possibly a homestead of the Macdonald family, provides some description of the terrain, and has names written on the blocks—a whole new field to investigate, with a new range of propositions.

Rate books are the last to check as manuscript migraine threatens, not to mention the imminent closing of the Public Record Office door for the day. The Moorabbin rate books are listed and a quick flick through the first one dated 1862 shows the conscientious clerk has listed the ratepayers with street addresses and with the type of dwelling they owned. The following year a new and less disciplined hand has only addressed those near the creek as 'Mordialloc' with unspecified 'freehold'. J.S. Parker and William Coleman (the selector's father) are both noted in passing. There is some good stuff available there for detailed work on the township.

It is time to organise the mass of information gathered from the

Date	Land use and source of information, Mordialloc, 1839–1907					
	Fishing	Grazing	Aboriginal	Town	Timber	Agric.
1839	Thomas VPRS 2896					
1844		Macdonald VPRS 5360				
1851			Reserve VPRS 5360			
1855		P.R. m		Hotel m		Land Sales GG
1858	Chinese VPRS 2896			Store VPRS 625		
1861		Common GG				
1863				Town Streets m		
1865				School	VPRS 795	Mentioned VPRS 795
1867				Churches m		
1871						Selection VPRS 625
1873				Park GG		
1876-7	pier (m)			Rec. Reserve		
1882				GG R'way m		
1907						Small Holdings VPRS 795
		VPRS	Vic. Pub. Rec. S. number			
		m	map			
		GG	Government Gazette			

Note that these are the earliest known dates, so these activities and building could be earlier. For example, the railway station opened in 1881.

two institutions—the main library and the main archival organisation. It could be summarised in this way.

Interaction of primary and secondary sources

Let us cheat now and follow these themes showing the other sources, both primary and secondary, used. Beginning chronologically, the Aboriginals must have been there first. The very early exploration of that side of the bay has curiously received little attention. *The Atlas of Victoria* has a historical map showing Charles Grimes and Charles Robbins to have traversed the coast to the Yarra in 1803, but Grimes makes no mention in his diary of the Mordialloc Creek. Secondary sources such as K. Bowden's *The Western Port Settlement and Its Leading Personalities* and N. Gunson's *The Good Country: A History of the Shire of Cranbourne* refer to Hovell's explorations around Westernport on an expedition there in the summer of 1826–27. Both books make tantalising mention of Hovell walking through to Port Phillip, but both writers are concerned with the more eastern excursions Hovell made at the time. Hovell's *Journal* is kept in the Mitchell Library in New South Wales and can be read in photostated form. From this it is quite clear that Hovell set off for Port Phillip in mid February, crossed a large marsh with great difficulty, and rested for the night on the beach.

Hovell's *Journal* records the following for 19 February 1827:

> ... a little after six sun time commenced [our] march along the beach towards the head of the bay, and at 8 o'clock came to a small outlet for water, which on following up a short distance, I found to be rather a broad and deep river and a small creek from the Marsh into it [a short fork]. After crossing stopped to breakfast and shortly after, nine of the natives paid us a visit unarmed. After a long gossip and a great deal of talk, not a word of which I could understand they took their leave, first giving each of them a fishing hook and about this same time, 11 o'clock I left also. From this time till nearly 1 pm the land fronting the sea gradually rose till it got to the height of about 200 feet perpendicular, the sea immediately under, and continued the same undiminished height till nearly the end of this day's journey but those parts which are the highest are generally the worst land, most of heath, no trees growing in it, the other parts are mostly good soil, but no large trees growing on it, only forest oak and honeysuckle. The grass although not thick, is good and fresh but there appears to be a great deficiency of water. This perhaps is owing to my keeping so near to the coast.

So there is a fascinating find. Eight years before John Batman 'purchased' the land around the Yarra from the Aboriginals, William Hovell breakfasted at Mordialloc, climbed the rise north of the district and continued along the coast through what is now Mentone,

Beaumaris and Sandringham. 'Oak' and 'honeysuckle' need careful deciphering. It seems likely that 'oak' refers to trees of the genus *casuarina*, or sheoak, a name derived from its timber, which has the fleck-like figuration of English oak but is considered generally inferior to that of its namesake, hence the sexist prefix. 'Honeysuckle' is not the fragrant yellow climber of English cottage gardens but the haggard banksia, the nectared cones of which sweetened the drinks of Aboriginal and white man like honey.

The following day Hovell and his party spent the night on the creek three-quarters of a mile (1.2 km) from its entrance, and the next morning followed it up until it dissipated into the marsh. They then returned along the Creek and breakfasted again at Mordialloc. Here they shot

> two very large birds, they appeared something between a Crane and Native Companion, are about the size of the latter, plumage slate colour, the head is devoid of feathers, but covered with a dark red smooth flacky substance, coarse black hair under the throat and a long straight dark green beak, flesh rather coarse, but good eating when made into broth.

It does not need much bird book reading to identify the birds as brolgas (*Grus rubicunda*), Australia's only crane. Hovell then moved off south along the beach where the party met 'a very large tribe of natives ... more than 100 men, women and children'.

There is no map with Hovell's journal so it is difficult to decide precisely where he was all the time. Distances are estimated, the countryside described, and compass points given. With much work, some reconstruction could be done. Nevertheless continual ferreting pays off and the map catalogue of the NSW archives has one notated Westernport. It is Hovell's map of 1827 and could be viewed on the microfiche, from which we can get a copy. The copy is a puzzle: Hovell's travels are marked with lines of dots and there seemed to be some tracks on the map unaccounted for in his journal. The other disappointing feature was a dark shadow that obscured the corner of the map where Mordialloc is now situated. On the original map (permission necessary to view), Hovell's tracks are in a different colour from the extraneous dots, and it is clear that these other dots represented not the path of Hovell's explorations but the estimated boundaries of the marsh through which he had struggled. His notation around Mordialloc was also legible with the help of a magnifying glass, reading: 'patches of heath surrounded by high stringy-bark trees'. This gives us the opportunity to glimpse Mordialloc

---

16 (*Overleaf*) William Hovell's map of Westernport, dated March 1827. Original held by the Archives Office of New South Wales.

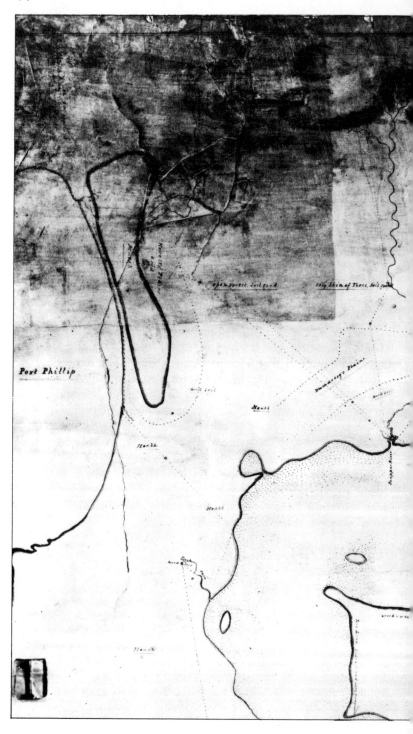

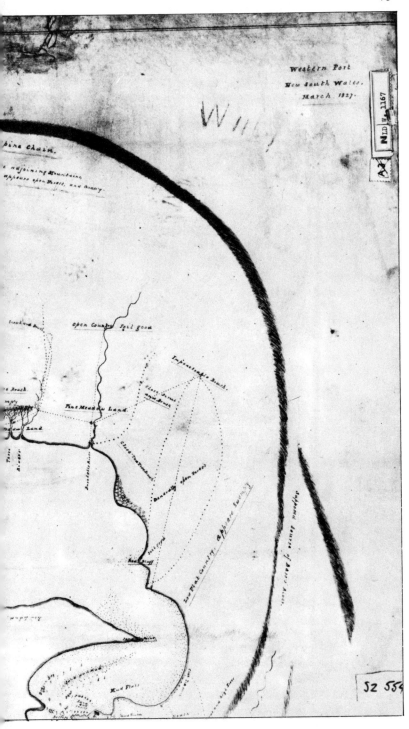

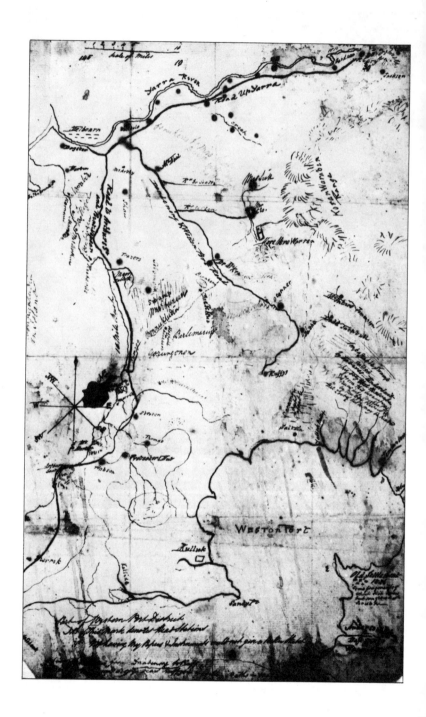

as it was, untouched by the white man's arrival. Hovell's shot reverberates down the decades.

William Thomas's manuscripts also at the Mitchell Library form 26 volumes of material and include the map reproduced. His journal and papers for the four years he spent with the local Aboriginals offer invaluable information from a concerned and sympathetic observer, some of which has been published in *Victorian Historical Records* (ed. M. Cannon, vol. 2A). Thomas's comments designate the Mordialloc Creek as part of the Bunurong tribe's domain, and in particular of a smaller band named the Kurrun. They called the mouth of the creek Moody Yallock, meaning 'high, high water' (Item 14, p. 173, p. 180), an interpretation which differs from the secondary source consulted (p. 56). Thomas writes of this place as being a favourite fishing spot of the Aboriginals and it is likely from the frequent references to eeling that the Aboriginals gathered there in autumn as the eels made their annual migration to the sea to spawn; in fact, it could well have provided enough food at this time for a meeting of the whole tribe with accompanying festivities, thus investing the place with considerable significance (p. 33).

Thomas first crosses the creek in 1839 following a trail (a likely forerunner of the Nepean Highway) blazed by the local Aboriginals at the request of Hobson, the only squatter ensconced at Arthur's Seat further down the bay. Thomas meets Major James Fraser who squats on the creek in 1840 with his Scottish family, mainly attractive daughters (census of 1841) in a homestead which probably passed to Macdonald three years later. He runs cattle.

Horace Wheelwright set up his camp on the hill in Mordialloc in 1853 after he came to Victoria in search of gold and decided that being a fowler for the Melbourne market was more to his liking. He was there for about five years and in 1861 he published *Bush Wanderings of a Naturalist* describing his life. Naturally it is an excellent source of information on the wild life, birds and vegetation around Mordialloc and across to Westernport Bay. He describes 187 species of birds, of which ornithologists can recognise 178. Wheelwright exemplified a European perception of the landscape, writing of 'a monotony of the scenery ... which is very wearying to the eye'.

During this time he saw more than two-thirds of the existing Aboriginals 'swept by disease and intemperance'. Interestingly he does not mention the Chinese, although he comments that 'a regular canvas town of fisherman's tents mushroomed between September

---

17 William Thomas's map of Port Phillip and Westernport, c. 1840. ML MSS 214, item 22, p. 547. Mitchell Library, Sydney.

and Christmas, when some forty or fifty boats fished the schnapper ground at the same time'. This may indicate the arrival of the Chinese just before he left in the late 1850s. Nor does he say much about the timber-cutters mentioned in the school file we saw. It would seem that they were at work on the 'forest oak and honeysuckle' described by Hovell, as both were in demand for furniture-making, and the sheoak for its smokeless fires much desired by bakers (Calder, W., *Mornington Perspective*, Melbourne, 1975).

The Titles Office

We do not know what happened to the Chinese and the timber-cutters who stayed at Mordialloc, or how long they stayed. We do know what happened to squatting. The run file shows Macdonald trying to transfer the rest of his lease in 1860 without success and then the common is declared and presumably Macdonald has by now retreated to the land he bought outside Mordialloc, until he dies in 1881 leaving the farm to his wife. The search note at the Titles Office makes this quite clear, and also reveals that Macdonald sold 150 acres in the south-west corner to Mary Munro in September 1858 for £300. Apparently she was his mother-in-law. William McLorinan had the title searched in 1895 and the rate books show that he then bought all the land which he subsequently sold to the Crown for the Small Holdings scheme responsible for the establishment of the Braeside school (Allot. 1, Sect. 22).

This Small Holdings or Closer Settlement land division can now enter the realm of oral history if you can find some children whose parents farmed there. Land files probably exist but, as yet, they defy the searcher. They would make an interesting and compact study. Now the land comprises the Braeside industrial estate, as industry has spread out from the back of Mordialloc.

Rate books

But that is getting ahead of ourselves. What happened to the selectors, the other farming group? Like Macdonald, they figure in the rate books, which are those of the old Dandenong Shire which included this area at the time. The rate books list the names in the nineteenth century, so it is not hard to follow the selectors through the years. By 1887 Hugh Brown has passed his allotment on to Thomas, Arthur and Frederick Brown while Robert Brown retains his. Coleman, McMahen and Ozanne have sold to Aaron Waxman whose occupation is given as broker, Rawlings, Owens and McSwain to F.D. Pearson, J. Staples and R. Inglis as a group. Three people as co-owners suggest either a family relationship, as with the Browns, or some sort of syndicate. This is 'land-booming' time in Melbourne and this small sample hints that much of the swamp land may have been sold to land speculators. Further work on the rate book confirms this supposition, and colouring in the land buys of the various syndicates on a map of the swamp shows the pattern up beautifully: not surprisingly, they concentrate on buying the land along the railway line which went from Mordialloc to Frankston in 1882. Of course in the 1890s the speculators go bust and it is not until that decade that some actual market gardening really gets going.

Parliamentary Papers: a Select Committee

But the question about how the selectors obtained their land if they did not live on it or grow crops in defiance of the Land Act regulations is solved by checking the index to Parliamentary Papers for material relevant to Mordialloc. Here is the report of a Select Committee appointed 'to enquire into . . . an alleged promise made to certain selectors . . . by virtue of which they selected land in the locality of the Carrum Swamp' (1876, vol. 1, no. 12). The Committee takes evidence and concludes that the selectors had been promised exemption from the residence clause because of the constant flooding. It is obvious that the drainage scheme, while going ahead, was not well enough advanced to encourage cultivation. The Lands Department therefore leased to the selectors even if they had not lived or worked the allotments.

Summary of the sources used

As for the town, this also goes ahead in the 1880s, to judge from the estates being broken up into streets and being sold with extravagant prose on the real estate agents' posters. Macdonald's hotel and Owen's store in the 1850s and the Bridge Hotel in the 1860s presumably survived on the fishing industry and the travellers who passed down the bayside, until the railway opening in 1881 causes a flurry of activity and introduces Mordialloc's next main use—its popularity for the tourist intent on a day at the sea or up the creek, an attraction which extends through the first half of the twentieth century.

There have been other uses not covered here. J.S. Parker's land, which is taken over by the Epsom racecourse, is outstanding. Nor have we dealt with the jetty's existence or individual township allotment sales. To be honest, they are more elusive than some of the material uncovered, and we have taken up enough space going so far.

To summarise briefly—the primary sources recommended at the beginning of this chapter in the section on land patterns, and which have been consulted in the research on Mordialloc, were a squatting-run file, parish plans, land-auction posters, a Titles Office search note, rate books, school files and the plotting of land speculators on our own map of the swamp. The patterns show Aboriginal use, squatting run, common, township and land sales, land selection under the 1869 Act which is not successful, land-booming and resale to new settlers for market gardening once the drainage is efficient. Feet-on-the-ground primary sources include an explorer's journal and map (Hovell), a contemporary diary and map of early 1840s (Thomas), a book of reminiscences of the area in 1850s (Wheelwright), land files (1870s) and parliamentary records (the 1876 inquiry into the swamp selectors). Together they give quite a comprehensive view of the district and its early inhabitants.

Some sources not tapped but which would add to this picture were the parliamentary debates (sure to feature the selectors' dilemma), early gazetteers (such as the 1865 one mentioning a post office and a four-horse coach passing through), the Select Committee's *Report on the Fishing Industry* in the Parliamentary Papers of 1892/93 (D2 and D5), and an army ordnance map for the 1920s (1:63,360). We did not go to the Lands Department at all but, if we had, we would have found supporting material: an early map of the whole area dated 1840, and Purchas's map of the Settled District around Melbourne in 1853 which shows the Aboriginal reserve quite clearly, early surveyors' maps of the Carrum Swamp, and a coastal survey by Commander Henry Cox which shows the hotel and a few houses in 1862.

Pictures and photographs

Before we finish this practical exercise, just a brief look at some of the pictorial material available. A visit to the picture collection of the Melbourne Public Library and a request to see the postcards of Mordialloc elicited a pair of white gloves for careful handling of the cards and five photograph albums of the modern sticky back and clear 'contact' variety (not a recommended way of storage but the way in which they arrived at the Library). These contained a seductive variety of early postcards including a dozen or so of Mordialloc, as well as some other cards in plastic covers, mostly more recent to judge from the cars. The latter were better presented because you could see both sides of the card, and a couple of early ones in plastic covers could be dated, thanks to the correspondent, and in turn helped to place some similar cards in the album.

The creek and the Bridge Hotel were the most popular subject for the cards. The creek was the subject of two very old photographs by the eminent Victorian photographer, Nicholas Caire, both of which give a good idea of its vegetation. One of the best postcards (Meade Album 6) showed a boat in the foreground and buildings on its bank. With the aid of a magnifying glass, it was possible to identify Mrs Redston's Bay View Dining Rooms and pick out advertisements on nearby buildings for hot and cold water, bait and stables. One building without advertisements dominated the centre of the post-card: it was a long house attractively faced by a seven-posted verandah and low picket fence. Along the road between this house and the creek were three sets of circular tree guards, presumably protecting three invisible trees. This postcard, from the look of it, dates from the first decade of the twentieth century. It testifies to Mordialloc's attractions for the tourist and the locals' readiness to benefit from them and to put some effort into improvements. It is possible to work out the position of the Dining Room and the adjacent house from another postcard (Album 2) which looks north from the main bridge in the foreground and shows them, on close examination, to the west. Today that would position them on the curve of road which sweeps from the Nepean Highway around into Beach Road. The Dining Room would indeed have had 'bay views'.

The small picture collection holds a neat watercolour of the Bloxsidge's (Bridge) Hotel by William Tibbits. It gives some impress-ion of the town about 1885, spring-cleaned though the landscape may be. Topographically the hotel sits on what is obviously a fork in the creek (described first by Hovell), the main stream winding away under a biggish bridge. The township is on the same side with its two churches, and this all agrees with present-day geography except that the fork (the Blind Creek) no longer exists. The recreational activities have not changed much—people still fish but there are now far more boats.

Useful historical information consists of the view of the two churches, the existence of a train, and the publican's name on the roof of the hotel. Textural detail for describing Mordialloc at that time would be the architecture of the hotel with its striped and coloured verandah roof, chimneys, steps and outbuildings, the way the bridges are constructed, the thin scattering of houses and the smoke from the steam train. Queries arise—Why is the name on the roof? What is the flagpole used for? Does the answer to both lie in communicating with passing ships? Was the garden of the hotel

18 Bloxsidge's Hotel, Mordialloc, Victoria, c. 1885. The original watercolour by W. Tibbitts is mainly in soft greens and yellows. La Trobe Library, State Library of Victoria.

designed with exotic plants or is that a result of Tibbits drawing native vegetation with English eyes? Actually the town area is surprisingly bare of trees.

Tibbits had been a painter, lithographer and engraver in England before he came to Victoria about 1865. It is suggested by a relative, George Tibbits (*Journal of the Royal Historical Society of Victoria*, vol. 54, no. 1, 1983), that William may have had some tuition in architectural drawing, so we can rely with some confidence on the detail in the painting. Much of the work he did was commissioned, some of it to illustrate land auctions, so he had a vested interest in making the residences and their surroundings appear as attractive as possible.

Tibbits follows the conventions of the 'picturesque' school of painting with figures and foliage in the foreground, the main subjects in the middle, with hills and clouds on the third level. Such conventions may have dictated an emphasis on the S-bend of the creek, and also the elevation of the furthest church to balance the middle level of the composition. It seems unlikely that Tibbits would have in fact been able to see the far church, which in reality is situated on the down side of the hill and would probably have been at least partly concealed from view at this position on the creek. Of course it may have happened that Bloxsidge persuaded the artist to advertise subtly the nearness of his hotel to both the railway station and churches.

Jumping ahead to the twentieth century and NATMAP, we find aerial photographs of Mordialloc are available only as early as 1945. These show a reasonably well-developed seaside town with houses dwindling away from the shore. The Epsom racecourse appears on the right of the photograph. Anybody familiar with Mordialloc today would immediately comment on its growth and extension since the photograph was taken. Most dramatic has been the change to the east of Mordialloc on the Braeside block which in 1945 consisted of a few farmhouses and now, zoned industrial, is rapidly filling with light industry.

3

People

Few of us have famous forebears of the sort which figure in most histories, the explorer, the squatter or early colonial politician, but we might have an obituary carefully cut from a country newspaper which speaks of great grandma's devotion to her family and her dedicated service to the church, or a portrait of careworn faces, or simply a desire to find out more about our ancestors. Australians are no longer afraid to find convicts rattling their leg irons in cupboards, and genealogy is providing a fascinating start to exploring the past for increasing numbers of people. At the same time the academic historian has sought to explore the lives of ordinary men, women and children in a move away from the former emphasis on the elite and on VIPs. With these developments comes the opportunity for the individual researcher to use some of the academic expertise to set his or her family members in relation to other members of the community and to appreciate some of the currents of economics and politics which carry people with them. At the same time again, the local historian is being pressed to relate her/his own particular patch of the world to its region as well as to State and national movements rather than to isolate it behind shire or city boundaries. The purpose of this chapter is to look at ordinary people's lives and to suggest some ways in which both their individuality and their interdependence can be researched and expressed.

THE ABORIGINAL PEOPLE

The Aboriginals were the first people in this country, and any study which sets out to tell the history of a particular place may well wish to reach back in time to the lives of the Aboriginals. An immediate problem presents itself: we have little record of their life before the white man arrived. Much of the evidence is pieced together from the work of archaeologists whose excavations of camp sites in coastal dunes, rock shelters and other likely places has encouraged an interest in what is known as prehistory—Aboriginal history before written records. So far very few of the Aboriginal sites identified have been studied in detail and if some excavation has been done in your research area, you should go straight to the archaeological reports for information. If this period interests you, some State archaeological offices run short courses and encourage amateurs to join the practical fieldwork.

Because so little material survives being buried under the ground for centuries, the other way to build up a picture of this presettlement life is to make tentative use of the existing records. These accounts come from the people who first met and lived with the Aboriginals in the early decades of settlement, such as explorers and squatters. Sometimes we assume that such early observations of Aboriginal life describe also the Aboriginal culture before the British arrived in Australia. But this arrival had an immediate effect on the Aboriginal patterns of life, for example, by probably forcing the Aboriginal bands to move more often around the hunting grounds as a response to the increased competition for food from the settlers and their animals. In 1839, only four years after the settlement on the Yarra River, the more obvious changes in tribal life are being noted by professional observers, such as William Thomas, assistant protector of the Aborigines in that area.

Indeed it has been suggested that the Aboriginal population was affected by fatal European diseases spread from a few places on the coast to much of the interior several decades before most Aboriginals had even seen or heard of the white man. This throws doubt on population figures based on the counts of the inland explorers. More importantly, it may mean that a drastic reduction in the Aboriginal population had taken place before their contact with the white man, and that this, in itself, could have changed the Aboriginal way of life. If you can imagine what it would be like suddenly to lose several members of your family and some friends or business associates, you will have some idea of the disruption that may well have taken place in the Aboriginal societies. So we cannot be sure that European descriptions of Aboriginal life, however soon they were made after contact, apply accurately to presettlement Aboriginal tribes. Moreover, we still have to allow for the bias and misconceptions of people from one culture trying to explain the life of a completely different culture. The British simply did not understand the semi-nomadic lifestyle of the Aboriginals.

Another common assumption still made in researching early Aboriginal societies is that their members lived in the same way, if not over all Australia, then certainly over all of what now constitutes a State. Yet the boomerang which is so strongly associated with the Aboriginal was unknown to some, to the Tasmanian Aboriginals, for instance, and unused by some South Australian tribes. There were many such differences: because there were creeks in an area, it does not automatically follow that the local Aboriginals made canoes, or that because there were reeds they wove nets. Unless the archaeological or very early written records specifically mention such activities, it is not possible to assume that the local Aboriginals behaved as their neighbours across the bay or the river did. They may, and they may not have done so.

DEMOGRAPHY

Demography is a study of human populations and examines both the structure of a population, that is, the age, sex, marital status, occupation, level of education, religious affiliation and so on of members, and the changes in the composition of the population brought about by births, deaths and migration. The demographer uses statistical measurement and mathematical methods but is not merely concerned to collect these figures but also to analyse and explain them. For this reason, demographic analysis is much used by sociologists and, increasingly, by historians.

Putting figures into tables, graphs and charts is a useful way of presenting statistics because this graphic presentation enables you to make comparisons and to appreciate differences easily. As illustrations, they show a lot of information quickly and clearly in a small space. They should always be carefully labelled and the source of the figures given. An example of a simple table is on p. 89.

The census

A count and questioning of the whole population over a brief period, or census as it is called, provides the main basis for demographic research. The Aboriginal population was excluded from the Australian census until legislation in August 1967 ended that exclusion, and then demographic estimates back to June 1961 were revised to include Aboriginals. (Estimating the Aboriginal population before the European's arrival, as already suggested, is a controversial matter, and if you are concerned with this, it is best to seek the latest information from secondary sources and your State Archaeological Office.)

First attempts to take a total count of the European population were called musters and they were not noted for their success. 'The correctness of these returns is not implicitly to be depended on,' wrote Governor Darling in 1827, and he was right. The following year an Act legitimised the taking of a census, and the return of the 1828 NSW census lists the colony's inhabitants in one alphabetical sequence, recording name, age, whether free or bond, the ship and year of arrival, sentence (if convict), religion, employment, residence, land and stock owned. The original manuscript returns were usually destroyed but do exist in some cases, for example, the returns for the 1841 census of the Port Phillip District (Victoria) still exist, signed by the head of each household. The members are not named, but information was required on the sex, age group, marital status, religion, occupation and whether free settlers or convicts. This means that if you know something about a household, for example, that the family consisted of a man, his wife, three daughters and a baby son, it is not hard to distinguish three single men aged between 35 and 45 as the shepherds, if you juggle the other categories.

From 1851 all colonies were required to take a census, which they did at different times, requesting different information. In 1890 a conference adopted a uniform procedure of collecting information and presenting it, subsequently carried out in 1891. Since 1911 the Commonwealth has been responsible for censuses and they have been carried out in 1921, 1933, 1947, 1954, 1961 and after that at five-year intervals. Table 2 shows the sort of information requested at these dates.

Although the local historian cannot examine individual census returns, a mass of detailed information can be gleaned from published returns. Census officials have usually based their statistical information on local government areas, and this allows comparisons over long time spans. Nonetheless, be wary, for local government areas do change their boundaries, and may not correspond from one census to another. Such changes can be checked in a municipal directory (see p. 53).

Population movements

Statistical information can show whether the long dray ride undertaken by grandfather William was part of a stream of men doing the same thing driven by the same incentive, or a maverick journey undertaken by a venturesome spirit. Or it could answer the sort of

Table 2 Some of the particulars obtained by Commonwealth censuses, 1911–1981

	1911	1921	1933	1947	1954	1961	1966	1971	1976	1981
Age	+	+	+	+	+	+	+	+	+	+
Birthplace	+	+	+	+	+	+	+	+	+	+
Nationality	–	+	+	+	+	+	+	+	+	+
Length of residence in Australia	+	+	+	+	+	+	+	+	+	+
Race	+	+	+	+	+	+	+	+	+	–
Religion	+	+	+	+	+	+	+	+	+	+
Education	Literacy/Illiteracy			–	–	–	+	Level completed Level attended		
Schooling	+	+	+	–	–	–	+	+	+	+
Marital status	+	+	+	+	+	+	+	+	+	+
Occupation	+	+	+	+	+	+	+	+	+	+
Occupation status	+	+	+	+	+	+	+	+	+	+
Unemployment	+	+	+	+	+	+	–	+	+	+
Income	–	–	+	–	–	–	–	–	+	+
War Service	–	–	+	–	–	–	–	–	–	–
Work force figures	–	–	–	–	–	–	+	+	+	+
Usual major activity	–	–	–	–	–	–	+	+	–	–
Dwellings										
Class	+	+	+	+	+	+	+	+	+	+
Materials	+	+	+	+	+	+	+	+	+	–
No. of rooms	+	+	+	+	+	+	+	+	+	+
Type of occupancy	–	+	+	+	+	+	+	+	+	+
Weekly rent	–	+	+	+	+	+	+	–	+	+

Note: This table does not provide a complete coverage of the information available from the censuses, and it should be remembered that the exact wording of the questions has not been the same from census to census. Race is based on a geographical rather than an ethnological definition.

problem posed by the dialogue reported by the Victorian Commission on State Banking (Parl. Papers, 1894–95, vol. 3) with a grazier from Yarrawonga:

9005. Was that particular piece of land that you have in your mind's eye bought up by a neighbour or sold to a new man in the district?—Sold to a new man.
9007. Are the farmers practically the same old hands that were here years ago?—There are exceptions.
9008. In connexion with the young men of the district, do you notice any tendency today on their part to take up their fathers' work and carry on the farms?—In some instances.
9009. Speaking generally, what do you think?—They have no other place to go. They have to take up their fathers' interest or leave the district.
9010. Do they do it out of choice, or is it a case of 'the devil driving'?—A good many have gone from here to New South Wales.
9011. Is farming popular with young men in the district?—There is no choice; they cannot turn their attention to anything else.

Let us look at two examples which use census figures to help us understand life and population movements in two different areas. The first concerns the Victorian cities of Bendigo and Eaglehawk. Table 3 shows the population changes in those cities between 1871 and 1901. The information is taken from the Victorian Census of the years listed and the percentage change is calculated by dividing the change in the population by the previous population multiplied by 100 over 1, as in

$$35\,584 - 28\,577 = \frac{7007}{28\,577} \times \frac{100}{1} = +25.5$$

Table 3   Population of Bendigo and Eaglehawk, 1871–1901

	Males	Females	Total	% Change
1871	15436	13141	28577	
1881	17851	17733	35584	+25.5
1891	16723	17366	34089	− 4.2
1901	18813	20328	39141	+14.8

Source: Victorian Census 1871, 1881, 1891 ad 1901

If long-term trends are required it may be more appropriate to plot the information graphically. Diagram 1 presents the same information set out in Table 3 for Bendigo and Eaglehawk males and females in a simple graphical form.

How can these population changes be explained? In the table we can note the dramatic increase in the population of Bendigo and Eaglehawk between 1871 and 1881. This corresponded to an increase

Diagram 1   Bendigo and Eaglehawk Population, 1871–1901

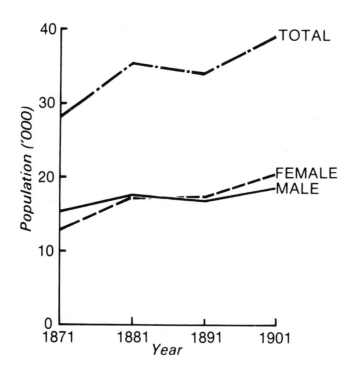

in quartz mining in the early 1870s. By the late 1880s the same quartz mines had declined, and it would seem the population migrated elsewhere in search of employment. During the 1890s Bendigo mines experienced a short revival and, with depression in Melbourne, possibly people were attracted back to the goldmining cities. From Diagram 1 we can see that in the early days of Bendigo, when it was a raw mining town, males outnumbered females. By the 1880s the gold diggers had settled down to the task of rearing families, and males and females were found in almost equal numbers. However, as the goldfield began to decline, young men left in search of employment. As a consequence women, by the turn of the century, outnumbered men.

Our second example, Diagram 2, shows Victoria's Wimmera shire in 1891 with a total population of 5124 and its distribution by age and sex. The age–sex distribution of a population can be most clearly presented in a graphical form called by demographers an age–sex pyramid. Thus the pyramid shows the total number of males aged five

Diagram 2   Age–sex pyramids, population of Wimmera, 1891

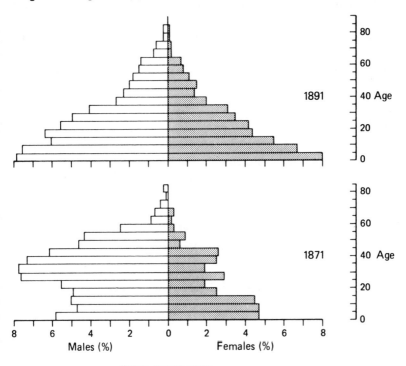

Source: Victorian census

to nine as 392 or 7.6 per cent of the total population of Wimmera in 1891.

These age–sex pyramids can reveal much about changes in the quality of life in a district. In 1871 the shire of Wimmera was dominated by squatters on large pastoral leases. In this environment there was not much scope for family life. Squatters found it cheaper to employ single males rather than married men with families. Accordingly an age–sex pyramid for 1871 shows that, in age groups twenty years through to 60 years, males far outnumbered females. There were also few children in the district. However, in the 1870s the squatters' sheep runs were thrown open for selection as farms, and this influx of settlers is reflected in the age–sex pyramid. By 1891 farmers had settled in the shire, with their wives and children, and the imbalance of adult males was less pronounced. Furthermore a large proportion of the shire's population was aged less than ten.

Migration

As Australia's white population is the result of migration going back over almost 200 years, there is a special interest in the background of the settlers. The census has generally recorded the birthplaces of the residents of local government areas. (See p. 25 on local government.) Table 4, for example, shows the main birthplaces of Bendigo males compiled from the Victorian census of 1881.

Table 4   Birth place of Bendigo and Eaglehawk males, 1881

	Number	Per cent
Victoria	9806	55.04
Other Australian colonies	593	3.33
England	4036	22.65
Wales	142	0.80
Scotland	696	3.91
Ireland	1267	7.11
Other British countries	108	0.61
Germany	356	2.00
Other European countries	170	0.95
China	548	3.07
Other overseas countries	46	0.26
At sea	32	0.18
Unspecified	16	0.09
Total male population	17 816	

Source: Victorian census, 1881

Diagram 3   Birth place of Bendigo and Eaglehawk males, 1881

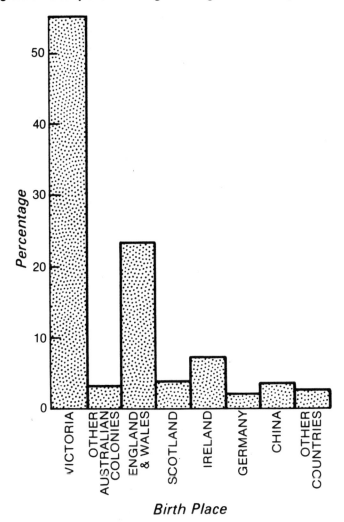

This information could also be presented graphically in a histogram as in Diagram 3. A histogram simply represents the percentage as bars and their relative size can thus be appreciated at a glance. It is quickly obvious, for example, that the biggest percentage of males were locals, born in the colony of Victoria, as represented by the largest bar.

It would be possible to compile a similar histogram for later dates, such as 1901 or even 1976, and to make a quick visual comparison of the changes in the proportions of migrants in those years. Having worked out the main ethnic groups, you can also use your raw statistics as springboards to other kinds of research, examining the Bendigo press to see how the minority of Chinese immigrants were received by the British majority, for example.

Crude birth and death rates

Civil registration of vital events, that is, of births, deaths and marriages, has been compulsory throughout Australia since 1856, although registration existed before this date. The demographer calculates the rates of these events in a population each year. They are commonly published as crude birth and death rates in government publications for selected districts in yearbooks and statistical registers. The crude birth rate measures the number of births per 1000 head of population, while the crude death rate measures the number of deaths per 1000 head of population. A further important measure is the infant death rate which measures the number of deaths of children under one year old per 1000 births in a year.

If these rates are not available for your particular district, they can be calculated if you have access to manuscript birth, death and marriage records (the volumes registering details of these events). At present such records are only open to university researchers under strict conditions of access which stress that the records must not be used to reveal details about individuals but rather to gather statistical data. Where access has been granted, crude death rates can be calculated in census years by simply counting the number of deaths and births. However before starting to use manuscript birth and marriage records you should take care to find out whether a registration district corresponds to the area counted in the census. In the City of Bendigo, for example, births and deaths could also be registered in adjoining hamlets, such as Eaglehawk and Kangaroo Flat, which were part of a different census area.

Armed with local birth and death rates you can begin to ask questions about your district. The historian of a suburb might ask whether his district was a less healthy place to live in than other suburbs, and whether the death rate rose with population increases. For example, the Melbourne suburb of Collingwood had a death rate of 20.5 deaths per 1000 head of population in 1881. This compared with only 7.9 for Victoria's country districts. It would seem Collingwood was a less healthy place than rural Victoria in which to live, and you could try to discover why this was so.

Age-specific birth and death rates

The chances of getting married, giving birth or dying vary, of course, with different people, which makes crude birth and death rates only rough, undiscriminating measures. When the local historian has access to official records, measures of birth and death can be refined by calculating birth and death rates specific to age and sex. For example, the age-specific death rate for males of a given age (or age group, such as 45–54) can be calculated by dividing the number of males who died at age x (or in age group x) by the male population aged x in that year. These rates can highlight aspects of life in a given locality. Thus, in 1891 when many men worked at quartz mining in Bendigo, the death rate in that city for women aged 45–54 was 29 and for men 62. Compare these figures with the respective rates for Victoria as a whole, which were 26 and 38, and it can be easily seen that gold was won at enormous cost to the men employed in the industry.

Family reconstitution and other sources

Family 'reconstitution' projects have drawn attention to other sources of information on births and deaths. Phillip Curson, while working on a family reconstitution project for St Phillip's parish in Sydney, explained the term: 'this technique is essentially the merging and organisation of a series of scattered records about the members of a family so that the demographic history of married couples and their offspring may be studied in detail in the context of the family setting.' The 'scattered records' to which he refers may be the press reports of local council health officers providing local death figures and cause of death. Or they may be records from local churches which kept copies of marriage certificates and baptism certificates, or those of local government bodies which recorded burials.

The family is traced from marriage through the baptism of the children, and passes from observation at the death of the last parent. When a family has been linked through all these records, such demographic details as the age at marriage of both the husband and wife, the number of children born to a couple, the number of children who died in infancy and the length of childbearing become known. Unfortunately the technique depends on the completeness of local records, and on whether parents bothered to baptise their children. Families who move out of the district further complicate such work. The method is enormously time-consuming, as the researchers,

186/1 .   **DEATHS in the District of** a *Forbes*

No.	When and where Died.	Christian Name and Surname, Rank or Profession.	Sex and Age	(1) Cause of Death. (2) Duration of last illness. (3) Medical Attendant. (4) When he last saw deceased.	(1) Christian Name and Surname of Father. (2) If known, with Rank or Profession. (3) Christian and Maiden Surname of Mother.	Signature, an Residence o
	Twenty first July 1871 *Forbes*	*Sophia Collett*	*Female 63 Years*	(1) *disease of heart* (2) *about fifteen years* (3) *none* (4) —	(1) *Edward Field* (2) *Farmer* (3) *unknown*	*John ?* *Son* *Forbe*

I, JACK HAYWARD WATSON, REGISTRAR GENERAL FOR THE ST

IS A TRUE COPY OF AN ENTRY IN A REGISTER KEPT AT THE

SYDNEY, N.S.W., AUSTRALIA.

19 Death certificate showing from left to right: place and time of death, name, occupation, sex, age, cause of death, names and occupations of parents, informant, registrar, place of burial and undertaker, date of birth, length of residence in the 'Australian colonies', place of marriage, age at marriage, wife's name, children's names and ages.

depending on the size of the district, will have to collect hundreds or even thousands of entries from marriage, baptism and death records before sorting these into family groups. It is quicker when access to official records has been granted. A recent study of Horsham in Victoria traced a number of families through local birth certificates from 1864 to 1899. These researchers were able to show that the original settlers in this district had families exceptionally large by modern standards. Women born in 1840–49 bore an average of eight children, and almost one-third produced a child after their twentieth year of marriage.

lony of *New South Wales.* Registered *by* ~~*James J. Wilshire*~~

	IF BURIAL REGISTERED.		Where Born, and how long in the Australian Colonies, stating which.	IF DECEASED WAS MARRIED.	
trict Registrar, rd.	When and where Buried, Undertaker by whom certified.	Name and Religion of Minister, or Names of Witnesses of Burial.		(1) Where and at what (2) Age, and to (3) Whom	Issue, in order of Birth, their Names and Ages
hive	24 *July* 1871 *Inhes*	*Fred McWilliams Church of England*	*Nepean*	(1) *Hartley* (2) 31 *years*	*three males four females living*
y 1871	*S. S. Her*	*Schulgirdham Philip Curry*	*lifetime in N.S.Wales*	(3) *James Pllett*	*one male deceased*

SOUTH WALES, DO HEREBY CERTIFY THAT THE ABOVE

GENERAL'S OFFICE. DATED 5th December, 1974.

REGISTRAR GENERAL. *Mee*

TRACING AN INDIVIDUAL

Researching an individual's life best begins paradoxically with that person's **death certificate**. This is because the certificate is essentially a summary of the important information about that life, providing the name, the age at death, the place of birth, the length of residence within the Colony, the parents' names, the mother's maiden name, the names of surviving children and often of the deceased children, and cause of death and the place of burial. This puts you in a position to seek a birth certificate by giving the approximate date of birth. A **birth certificate**, in return, will provide the birth places and occupations of the parents and the date and place of their marriage, as well as the names of their older children. A **marriage certificate** will provide the names of the parents as well as those of the bride and groom. In this way you can wend your way back at least to the country from which your individual's family came, at which stage investigation may become more complicated and you will need to seek advice. A death certificate also helps you to pinpoint the likely time of arrival within a colony and narrow the search for your subject in the **shipping records** at the public record office in the relevant State. These records generally provide age, occupation, religion, and information on whether the immigrant could read and/or write. In all States, except Victoria, indexes of births, deaths and marriages have been placed on microfiche and are readily available. In Victoria a request to the Registrar-General's Office, plus a fee, will provide a search through the records for the five years around a possible date. The accuracy of information on certificates is only as reliable as the knowledge of the 'informant', usually a relative, close neighbour, or good family friend, supplying the details.

If you do not have an exact death date, you may be able to find the individual in a directory of the town in which he or she lived. These **directories** contain alphabetical lists of the main householders' names and addresses, like telephone directories of today, and, similarly, they are heavily male-oriented. Sometimes the lists are geographic, that is, by street, and sometimes by trade or profession. The last time the name appears in a directory may indicate that your subject has died and thus give you an approximate date of death; equally, of course, it may just mean that he has moved. You could try a check with the local cemetery records about the time of the disappearance from the directory.

Fleshing out the bare bones takes some real work. Useful sources are **electoral rolls** for moves and occupations. Be careful: how many times have you changed your occupation since you first gave it to the electoral officer? Women, of course, did not vote in the nineteenth century. Other sources include **local histories, library biographical indexes** (enquire), **local newspapers** (laborious scanning unless indexed), **biographical publications**, and **occupational listings** such as those of politicians, doctors, dentists, teachers, police, lawyers, chemists, civil servants (ask your librarian again). At public record offices there are early **censuses, inquests, naturalisation indexes** and **indexes of wills**.

Bodies specifically organised to help are the **genealogical societies** in the telephone book; they have their own libraries and magazines. The Church of Jesus Christ of the Latter Day Saints (Mormons) also has genealogical libraries and impressive computerised records, including records from Britain. The genealogical societies can tell you how to consult the convict indexes and how to find the convict's trial or a description of the conditions on the ship's voyage to Australia and any records made on the convict's arrival. There are societies with a specific interest such as the Australian Railway Historical Society or the Military Historical Society of Australia who may hold information relevant to your inquiries.

Biographies and obituaries

Some biographical detail can be gained from obituaries in local newspapers and from celebratory volumes such as Sutherland's *Victoria and Its Metropolis* (1888). Normally these biographies will be concentrated on local notables such as councillors, but relatively obscure individuals also had their lives recorded. If the entries were provided and paid for by the subject, as was the case with *Victoria and Its Metropolis*, there is a chance that the biographies can be substantially relied on, although naturally the emphasis is on success. Obituaries, on the other hand, were compiled by local journalists talking to friends and family and are often wrong. They should be regarded as 'leads' only and, of course, as character reference they were often works of art in euphemism. The 'good businessman' who emigrated from Cornwall in 1861 may well turn out to have come from nearby Devon in 1864 and to have a reputation for making money in unscrupulous ways. In this way obituaries resemble the laudatory farewell dinner speeches which habitually accompanied the departure from the district of any male resident of note, a designation which might apply to anybody from the local bank manager to the railway-station master.

Diaries

To learn how people felt about vital events such as death, marriage, birth or migration, we must turn to diaries and letters. Diaries, of course, were not kept by all members of society, but in the nineteenth century they were often kept by the obscure as well as the powerful. Women, who are well-nigh invisible in other forms of documents, appear in the pages of diaries. Agnes Rose Field, the daughter of a Goulburn Valley selector, kept an account of her daily activities (MS at La Trobe Library, State Library of Victoria). On the first of January 1882 she wrote:

> This is my very new diary a present from my dear brother Tom and I prize it very much firstly because it was his present after his serious illness and secondly as it will be his last (I expect) as a bachelor for he has another now to claim his attentions and presents. Let us hope dear old diary that we will have nothing to note down in your pages that will cause pain. Let it

all be pleasant remembrances of days past never to return. Although we cannot expect to have all Sunshine in this world we like our share and hope we may get it.

Agnes Rose Field never married but her diary records the marriages of her brothers and sisters and the birth of their children. The diary also reminds us that people in our local district were not insulated from national affairs. For example on 18 April 1900 she observed:

> Our first sorrow came when Mat and Henry joined the Imperial Regiment to serve in the Boer War in South Africa. [They] left home today after having our photos taken. All went to the station with heavy hearts to see them off. There was a good many friends there who had been at the presentation the night before to bid them farewell. All were very sad when the train moved off with our soldier brothers whom we may not see on earth again, but hope to.

Her family was also touched by the great migration of eastern Australians to Western Australia.

High rates of child mortality cannot communicate the agony that families experienced with sick and dying children. Isaac Edward Dyason, a Bendigo Mine speculator, kept a daily diary for almost 50 years, now held at the La Trobe Library, State Library of Victoria. On 17 January 1891 Dyason noted that his eldest son Clarence (aged five) 'had an attack of fever begun with Monday['s] sunstroke'. By the nineteenth Clarence was 'lying patiently' but was 'as hot as fire'. On 20 January Dr Boyd was consulted and Clarence, who was as 'red as a lobster', was diagnosed as suffering from scarlet fever. The doctor advised that Dyason's two daughters—Emily and Amy—should not attend school for three months. However when Dyason returned from work that night he found the baby Cecil (aged 21 months) and Emily (aged 9 years) 'down with fever and bad in their throats, worst symptoms'. Although the elder children recovered, the baby grew steadily worse. The end came on 6 February:

> my poor baby sinking I feel, pray God spare him ... Office. Amy came for me to say Cecil is dying. Went over. Boyd there says there is a glimmer of hope, very faint. Poor little fellow weakening every hour slowly dying out exhausted ... baby swallowed last medicine about 7.30 then gasped for breath till 20 minutes to 11 saw him, wife with me, draw last breath Oh God.

Interviewing

Although personal written records and statistical sources are our main props in an examination of the lives of ordinary men and women in the nineteenth century, most of the twentieth century lies within living memory. Interviewing is a way of finding out about experiences of courtship, marriage, childbirth and death, if approached with tact and patience. No less delicate subjects are family relationships and attitudes to religion and politics, but most people will talk willingly on the two subjects to which we now turn—work and leisure.

WORK

The local historian has the chance to record methods of work which were once used in his/her area but which are no longer common or in existence; they may be those of herdsman, charcoal-burner or early worker in a canning factory. The depression and World War II brought new and sometimes harrowing experiences to people's lives and work. Some dramatic changes are comparatively recent. Consider, for instance, the transformation of the average dairy farm by tractor and milking machine since World War II.

Census information

You can place the accounts of the individuals to whom you speak within the broad patterns provided by analysing the census returns. The returns will reveal the occupational framework of a community, the differences in occupations between different places, and the changing work trends. In recent census publications occupational

Table 5   Occupation distribution for Bendigo, 1971

	Males	Females	Total
Professional	526	655	1181
Administrative	619	103	722
Clerical	517	868	1385
Sales workers	572	591	1163
Farmers	263	28	291
Miners	15		15
Transport workers	644	53	697
Craftsmen	3396	625	4021
Service workers	391	857	1248
Armed services	142	13	155
Other not stated	330	186	516
Unemployed	168	91	259

Source: Australian Census 1971

distributions are given for local government areas. Table 5, for example, gives the occupational distribution for Bendigo in 1971.

Compiling occupational distributions at different points in time can document vividly changes in a local area. In Bendigo in 1903 almost one-third of electors were miners, but by 1971 this once great goldfield had a mere fifteen men employed in mining. Occupational distributions could also be used to compare districts. Did neighbouring suburbs contain the same proportion of white-collar workers such as professional and clerical workers?

Although they did not use the same occupational classifications, occupational details were sometimes given in nineteenth-century and earlier twentieth-century census publications. When the census did not give occupational details, or you wish to look at a smaller area than that presented in the census (an individual street for example), you can resort to a rate book, to electoral rolls or to a directory to identify individuals and to match them with their occupations. This is possible on a small scale even if these present a large amount of detail that will need to be organised into occupational groups. Perhaps the simplest approach would be to adopt the classification employed by the recent censuses and shown in Table 5. Modern census publications such as a *Catalogue of the 1976 Census Tables* will give a guide to the type of individual occupations which belong in each broad groups, for example tradesmen includes bricklayers, plasterers and electricians, professionals includes doctors, lawyers and architects, while numbered among service workers are housekeepers, caretakers and laundresses. With lists of occupations from the nineteenth century the local historian will have to be aware of changes in the use of words. The term 'engineer' in the nineteenth century does not always refer to professionals such as civil engineers. More often it refers to skilled tradesmen such as fitters and turners.

Statistical registers

The census is not the only place to get statistical information about work in your district; most colonies, and later the States, published statistical registers annually. If your area of study is an agricultural district, the statistical registers will detail the numbers and types of livestock in your district, the size of farms, the area in crop, the type of crops sown and the yield of these crops. Simple graphs compiled from these statistics can illustrate in a striking way important historical changes in your district. Diagram 4 illustrates the soaring increase in wheat acreages that occurred in the County of Rodney in the years after the arrival of free selectors. For historians of urban

Diagram 4 Wheat acreage 1870/1 to 1900/1, County of Rodney

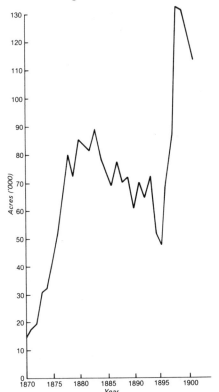

areas, statistical registers can be used to determine the number and type of factories in a suburb or town, and the number of 'hands' employed in such factories.

Parliamentary Papers

Valuable as they are, official statistics cannot tell us what it was like to work on a farm or in a factory, and again they should be interwoven with individual voices to remind us that these represent living and loving people. The minutes of evidence taken by royal commissions and published in Parliamentary Papers present oral history from the nineteenth century transcribed, and many are indirectly full of information about work. Often a seemingly unlikely investigation, into such topics as the fiscal system or the tariff, will contain details about local working conditions.

In the nineteenth century all colonies passed legislation to place farmers on the public estate. The efficacy of the various land laws was an obvious subject for parliamentary investigations, and is a windfall harvest for local historians. Similarly, the Victorian Commission into the Fiscal System travelled throughout Victoria collecting evidence from local farmers on the problems they experienced making farming pay. Other royal commissions dealt specifically with agriculture, such as the Victorian Commission on Vegetable Products (final report 1894) and the NSW Commission inquiring into 'Rural, Pastoral, Agricultural, and Dairying Interests' (1917–18).

Royal commissions also examined the working conditions of urban dwellers. The Victorian Inquiry into Shops in 1902 took over 900 pages of evidence in Melbourne and suburbs, Victorian provincial towns, and even in Sydney, Brisbane, Tasmania and New Zealand. This commission included an enormous amount of detail on working conditions, wages and hours. The following extract presents a portion of the evidence given by a Sydney baker, John Hawkins:

> 4297.   What effect has the adoption of the Factories Act had on your trade?—None.
> 4298.   Is there any sweating in your trade?—A tremendous lot. From nine to nineteen hours a day are the hours of labour. In a fair shop, nine hours is the proper amount per night; in the sweating shops, fifteen hours is about the average per night, and nineteen and twenty hours on Friday and Saturday. I speak as an employee, from practical knowledge.
> 4299.   What are the wages?—The union rate is from £2 10s. to £3 10s. a week; in the other shops, 25s., 35s., and up to £2.

Employers also gave evidence. Henry McCormack, of the metal merchants McLean Brothers and Rigg, was asked: What is the average rate of wages paid in your business? He answered:

> We pay generally according to the merits of the men. An employee, the manager of a warehouse, might get £500 a year. An employee may be in a warehouse twenty years, getting only 50s. a week, I know of some. That is where a wages board would not come in. Departmental managers average about £3 a week. When they enter the business, we give the boys 5s. a week to start with. As a rule, we take a boy for three years, though there are no indentures. We pay 5s. the first year, 7s.6d. the second, and 10s. the third year. After that he is paid what the employer considers he is worth. Before taking him on we have a month's trial on either side.

In the second half of the nineteenth century Australian governments sought to regulate the working conditions of employees in factories and mines. The annual reports of local factory inspectors and mining inspectors contain a wealth of information about local work conditions. The Ballarat inspector of factories included the following in his report on the state of trade in his district in 1906.

> The Government also spent £12,000 in the district, including £8,000 for alterations and additions to the Wendouree Asylum, whilst the remainder, £4,000, were spent in other buildings, thus providing employment to a number of local artisans.
>
> In the boot trade the hands were kept fairly well employed during the year, and I was informed by one of the principal manufacturers that his turn-over for the year exceeded £3,000 compared with the previous year, whilst another, also in a big way, told me that his returns were much better than the previous year.
>
> The fellmongers and tanners had not such a good year, and, in consequence, a number of the hands were compelled to take time off, especially amongst the dressing goods (tanners).
>
> One of my principal firms, who employ about 40 hands, had a record year in the manufacture of 'footballs,' viz 12,000, for I am told this is the highest output, and an inter-State trade is being done, including New Zealand.
>
> The underclothing trade still continues to prosper, and apart from local orders, a large business is being done with Melbourne also South Australia and Tasmania. Extra accommodation has had to be provided, and one of the finest 'up-to-date' factories has been built with a floor space of 10,000 square feet, capable of accommodating 250 workers.

In Victoria annual reports of the mines department provided not only details of gold yield but details of union membership, wages paid received by the various classes of labour in the mines, unemployment rates and sickness benefits paid to union members. From the mid-1870s to the 1890s detailed descriptions of mining accidents and the compensation paid to victims and their families were provided. Inspectors also reported on new machinery introduced and attempts to improve the working conditions in mines, by such means as ventilation shafts.

Industrial and business records

Above the ceiling in one of Echuca's old buildings were found the working records of one of the big shipping companies for the years from 1864 to 1883. These thousands of letters, pay sheets, shippers' logs, ships' manifests and Customs records with the old files of the *Riverine Herald*, enabled Allan Morris to depict the river trade of the Murray in his book *Rich River* (1953). Company records often include personal records on employees such as wages and engagement books. From these you can trace the fortunes of individual workers, or a number of workers, over a period of years and see whether they experienced periods of unemployment. You can also see from wages books the actual difference in wages between skilled employees, such as engineers, and unskilled labourers. Company minute books and union records, where they are available, are often rich sources. At a time of a local crisis, such as a strike, you could compare the different attitudes of the company and the strikers, if records survive. Local company minute books might also reveal a company's attitude to development in your district. Union records are also valuable for times other than strikes, for these bodies formerly provided social services such as sickness, injury and unemployment benefits.

Contemporary material

Local historians who find that local company and union records have been destroyed or lost can find a wealth of information in local newspapers. In Bendigo, for example, all miners' union records seem to have disappeared. Although this prevents the historian from examining membership of the union, its activities can still be followed in almost verbatim reports of union meetings published in the local press. Likewise Bendigo mining company records have all but disappeared. Again the local newspapers are very important, for they provide lengthy accounts of annual and half-yearly meetings. Often local companies will be private concerns and hence did not need to produce annual reports. In these cases the local press is still a useful place to look. Journalists were often sent to examine local works and to interview local businessmen. With the introduction of press photographs in the mid-1890s local newspapers often presented illustrated accounts of local shops, factories and mines. At times of strikes workers aired grievances about pay and conditions in letters to the editor and, of course, their employers sought to refute the union case. The views of local employers, on such issues as the tariff, also came in letters to the editor. The employers also appear making political speeches at dinners and before elections, all reported at great length.

A number of specialised journals focusing on a particular industry or trade appeared weekly or monthly, most from the 1880s onwards. Examples are the *Australian Miller*, the *Australasian Ironmonger*, the *Australasian Painter and Decorator*, and the *Australasian Builder and Contractor's News*. Books written on local industries vary from J.P. Dowley's *Dairying in Australia* (Sydney, 1888) to F. Danvers Power's *Coalfields and Collieries of Australia* (Melbourne, 1912), and there are many more for smaller regional areas, some of which have been reprinted.

Diaries

Diaries are an important source for examining local working conditions and attitudes between employers and employees. The Bendigo diarist we met earlier, Isaac Edward Dyason, for example, frequently wrote of the plight of miners and detailed disputes between miners and mine owners. On 8 June 1895 he jotted in his diary: 'lot of poor tributers [miners] coming in ab[ou]t 10/– a week to keep families on.' On 7 February 1880 he noticed 'some of [the] men at Colman's [mine] shirking work presuming on [their] knowledge of [the] working of [the] mine. Told the manager to discharge them ...' But it was not only employers and employees who argued. In 1881 Dyason wrote of a dispute involving three directors of the mining company: 'Bell in trouble at Carlisle meeting. Watson accuses him of being a tool in Lansell's—Bell in tears—great rough fellow—Sorry for him!'

In agricultural districts diaries were kept by farmers and their wives. Not surprisingly, considering the long hours they laboured, these diaries are laconic, simply enumerating the work done on each day. Typical of these was the diary of James Harris James of Jacklin in Victoria (held by the Pyramid Hill Historical Society).

September 30th 1890	Finished fallowing Heavy showers the ground very hard.
Oct 22	Darling to Stonewall Jackson [These are horses]
Oct 27	Finished shearing, Wool 8d, Lambs wool 6 ¾d.
Nov 10	Commenced Hay cutting. Little grasshoppers in millions everywhere.

The diaries sometimes include details of types of wheat sown by the farmer, and newspaper cuttings of advice from the agricultural press. When income tax was levied, annual earnings might be scribbled into diaries to be compared with later years.

Probate inventories

Details of agricultural work can also be inferred from the probate inventories compiled when farmers died (see pp. 134–5). The estate of Edmond Power, a farmer and grazier of Wycheproof, who died in

June 1901, gives some idea of his farm, agricultural equipment, and likely work schedule:

A Probate Inventory

Real Estate

1930 acres 3 roods 30 perches in the parish of Bunguluke, County of Kara Kara. Fenced with post and wire and chock and long fences. Improvements include five tanks and a homestead of weatherboard containing two rooms. Municipal Assessment £204 per annum Value £4342/10/–.

Personal Property

Crops

Hay Stack £5, 359 bushels of wheat 8/– per bushell £140/–/–.

Livestock

300 Comeback ewes with 80 percent lambs	13/–	£195.
300 Comeback ewes	10/–	£150.

2 geldings £13, 2 mares in foal £28, 1 gelding £13, 2 hacks £3, 2 pigs £3, 20 fowls £1.

Implements

1 winnower £3, Reaping Machine £1, Scoop £1, 1 triple furrow plough £1, 1 double furrow plough £1, 1 set of Harrows £1, 1 wool press £3.

1 waggon £10, 1 Dray £3, 1 spring dray £3, Harness £2.

Furniture

2 stretchers (bush made), 2 old trunks, 1 sofa dilapidated, 1 bedstead broken, 1 chair broken, a billy can, 1 table home-made, 1 stretcher, a table lamp, 2 cups and saucers, plates and a safe, and a few other kitchen utensils £5/17/6

A few old clothes worthless

Bank Deposit: Bank of Australasia Wycheproof £513/2/–.

LEISURE

Ask Australians ensconced before their television sets what they did before 1956, and you will be rewarded by vivid memories of school picnics, church concerts, cycling clubs, the illegal two-up game complete with lookout, singing around the piano, the day the circus came to town, the dances in the barn and the sleepy trip home with its reliance on an equally sleepy horse and the light of a full moon, not to mention fishing for leeches by dangling bare legs in the creek, 'chasing the greasy pig' and sundry other activities which need to be recorded now in all their warm-hearted, full-bodied immediacy.

Local institutions

Surprisingly, reminiscences about such events can be tapped through a request for information in the local paper about a local building. Illustrate it with a photograph, and stand by the telephone for the ready response. A dilapidated mechanics' institute, a commemorative plaque, or the ornate facade of a building once used by the Oddfellows friendly society but now used as a florist's shop can remind us of the social and religious institutions and meeting places once considered significant in the life of the people of our past. Many of these buildings are still in use: the town or shire hall, the masonic building, and the local churches; the mechanics' institutes, originally designed as halls for adult education in the nineteenth century, now appear in new dress as anything from social clubs to historical museums. The institutions were often a source of great pride to a local area; indeed they put a community on the map. Local or colonial centenary publications in the late nineteenth century provide the historian with what could be called a 'civic inventory': a list of those groups and organisations which, collectively, announced its identity. The list might be something like this:

> ... a Mechanics' Institute with a library of 13,000 volumes, and a free library of 2,292 volumes, each having a large hall fitted up for concert or theatrical purposes, with stage, scenery and other requirements. Other buildings are the Exhibition hall or Theatre ... a Homeopathic dispensary, Orphan Asylum and Female refuge. The churches are three Episcopal, two Roman Catholic, two Wesleyan, five Presbyterian, three Primitive Methodist, two Congregational, four Baptist, a United Methodist, and a Jewish Synagogue.

The number and variety of these organisations will depend to a large extent on the size and character of the locality you are studying; for example, there was little need for a suburban municipality to have an Agricultural and Pastoral Association. Similarly, in a mining town

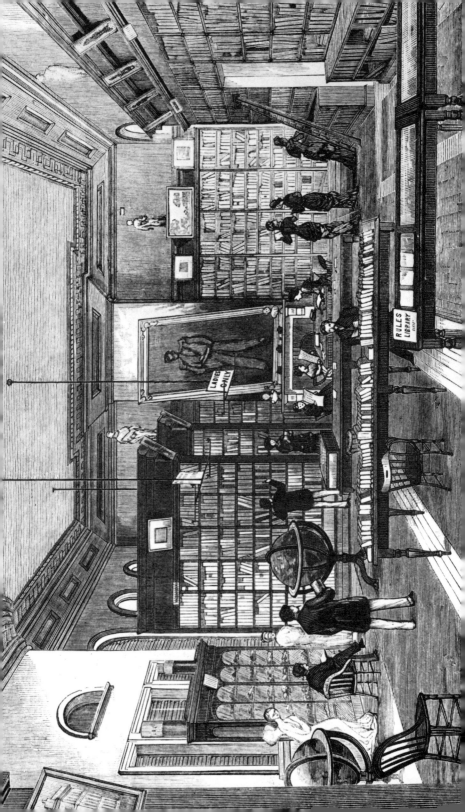

dominated by families from the English counties of Cornwall and Durham, you will find more Methodist chapels than Presbyterian or Anglican churches. A consideration of some of the basic characteristics of the community (using the sources discussed earlier in this book) should help you understand some of these variations or peculiarities.

As you proceed with your investigation, it may be worthwhile grouping these organisations and meeting places under general headings such as this:

> Church
> Civil improvement
> Culture
> Economic advancement
> Education
> Politics
> Social
> Sport
> Welfare

You should not regard these headings as indicating strict divisions in the function or purpose of activities, since you will soon realise that they often overlap. For example, church groups were actively involved in welfare organisations, such as orphan asylums, and in the provision of education. Friendly societies offered sickness and funeral benefits to their members but also provided opportunities for recreation. Nevertheless, a broad classification of groups in the community will help you organise your notes and ideas.

Local newspapers

The local newspaper is the indispensable source for information on community social life. All parts of a newspaper are useful for some purpose: announcements, advertisements, leading articles, letters to the editor, poems and brief descriptive items can all contain some details relevant to your research. Even announcements of the opening of subscription lists for a building fund can indicate the range of support available to an organisation.

20 Reading room, Ballarat Mechanics' Institute, woodcut from the *Australasian Sketcher*, 1881. National Library of Australia.

Annual reports are reprinted in the paper. For example, in 1860 the Williamstown Mechanics' Institute appended a list of lectures which had been delivered in that year. Together with the names of the lecturers and the topics of the lectures, this list also gives the estimated attendance at each lecture, a helpful source which one can use to assess the popularity of these activities. Annual reports often include the speeches of office-bearers or patrons which can show us how the fortunes of these groups rose or fell, and what role these institutions saw themselves performing in local society. (See also p. 106.)

Date	Lecturer	Topic	Estimated Attendance
19 July	J.S. Percival	The Rifle	175
2 August	Rev. E. Watkin	The Native War in New Zealand	300
7 August	Rev. W. Robinson	The Atmosphere	250
16 August	Rev. Dr. Bromby	The Eddystone Lighthouse	200
23 August	R.L.J. Ellery	Electro-Magnetism	200
30 August	J. Wallace	Phrenology	150

Speeches and processions on the occasion of the laying of foundation stones or the opening of buildings also disclose the aspirations of local groups and the participation of the population in general. For example, the day appointed for the opening of the Yass Mechanics' Institute was proclaimed a general holiday in the town. Flags and bunting festooned the street and the local brass band was accompanied by a peal of bells ringing out from St Clement's Anglican church. The Athenaeum at Kyneton was opened amid general rejoicing in October 1858, with the climax of the festivities being a dance to the 'Kyneton Athenaeum Polka', specially composed for the occasion by the local music professor. At the laying of the foundation stone of the North Melbourne Wesleyan church, the Reverend D.J. Draper pointed out that the church would 'constitute a prominent feature in the architectural ornaments of the city, the site being on the hill above the late cattleyards, from whence it will be visible to a considerable distance'. The architectural qualities of a building were often seen as being a material reflection of the importance of the people who were to use it, and the values they regarded as significant. Twenty-five, 50 and 100 years later there are sure to be celebrations with possible reminiscences.

In the newspapers you will find descriptions of ploughing matches and athletic sports which were part of the agricultural shows, the peak of the rural social calendar, and of national festivals such as the St Patrick's day celebrations. Horse races, football matches, theatrical performances, charity bazaars and many other occasions sponsored by local organisations led to extensive descriptive and mutual back-slapping accounts. But the newspaper can also indicate divisions and dissatisfaction in local communities, as much as cooperation and general enjoyment. Letters to the editor or the reports of meetings of district road boards and shire and municipal councils bring to light some of the issues contributing to local discord. Indeed, the paper could well provide the battleground on which local identities skirmished in print, much to the delight, no doubt, of the circulation-conscious editor, and the rest of the non-aligned residents.

If your aim is to develop a portrait of social life and the activities of local organisations in general, it is sensible to select a particular month of a year, or one particular year upon which to concentrate. This should generate enough information if you do not wish your study to be exhaustive. If you are tracing the history of a particular group then you will probably develop a technique of skimming the paper and concentrating on those sections which will give you the greatest amount of information. For example, a certain group, such as a hospital committee, may publish its annual report in the first week of September of each year, and it may appear regularly on page 3 of the newspaper. The easiest way of homing in on specific pieces of information is to use an index to the local paper, if one exists. Unfortunately this is rare, but some of the newspapers of the larger provincial towns have been indexed. Local historical societies have sometimes set to work and compiled a partial index to the files of the local paper; it is worth enquiring.

Journals of organisations

Many of the organisations which were active in your local area will have been affiliated with colony-wide or Australia-wide groups. A number of these produced journals and reports which may contain important supplementary material to the newspapers. The journals of religious denominations, such as the *Melbourne Church of England Messenger* and the *Messenger of the Presbyterian Church of New South Wales*, carry news of individual church activities. Other journals include those of the friendly and temperance societies. Occasionally the news of local events in these sources may be more detailed than that given in the newspapers, reproducing the contents of speeches and sermons. Conference reports and statistical material relating to religious denominations can be found in annual publications—these have titles such as the *Yearbook of the Diocese of Melbourne*, or the *Proceedings of the General Assembly of the Presbyterian Church of Victoria*. Some of the statistical tables in these sources can be useful to the historian in assessing the level of attendance at church services, debts on buildings, the amount of income derived from the renting of church pews and the stipends of clergymen. They can even include details of the attendance of Sunday School pupils.

Directories

Local directories will often list some of the main meeting places in an area. They include information such as the names of office-bearers, mayors, councillors and council officers, fees for sporting and cultural groups and times of church services. These advertisements give the date of an organisation's establishment. If the researcher is trying to find the geographical position of an institutional building that no longer exists, then the directory can perhaps provide this information. Remember that church buildings are not subject to local rates, so the rate books will not help if you are trying to locate a church, and the directory is a useful alternative.

Pamphlets

Pamphlet literature can also be a fruitful source. Pamphlets were often produced by local or government printing offices, and they may include lectures, reports, announcements, polemical debates or reminiscences. These can offer further evidence about the activities of organisations. The best way of finding these is through the catalogues of major libraries—the name of your locality will be the most useful subject heading to use. Other sources for early pamphlets include Ferguson's *Bibliography of Australia* (this is a 'union' listing as well as a bibliography, and indicates the main libraries in Australia

287.106	Maitland District
M	Methodist Church of Australia
	N.S.W.
	Quarterly directory of the West Maitland Circuit. Vol. 1, No. 4, May–Jy. 1892.

> | | Lillie, *Rev.* John |
> |---|---|
> | 374 | Opening Lecture of the session, on know- |
> | L | ledge as the means of correcting prejudice. |
> | | Delivered at the lecture hall of the Van |
> | | Dieman's Land Mechanics' Institution 8 vo. |
> | | pp. 34, Hobart Town, W. Pratt, Printer, 1843. |

where the item is held) or the published catalogue of the Mitchell Library, available in 38 volumes (plus supplement) in most State libraries. Above are some representative entries from the Mitchell Library Catalogue.

Records of organisations

One of the first things to look for is an existing history of the institution you are studying. This could be a large book or a jubilee booklet. Most churches have produced small **booklets** to mark 50 or 100 years of existence. This can save you some work if it is small pieces of information you need—the names of clergymen, trustees or leading lay people. Sometimes they include photographs of the congregation, Sunday School members or the interior of the church. Such booklets have also been produced by Masonic lodges, sporting organisations, scouts, schools, service clubs, business firms, and so on.

Many of these groups had their **annual reports** printed and circulated to members. Copies of these may survive either with the organisation itself, or in major libraries or historical societies. (See also p. 112.) They will list the current office-bearers and sometimes provide lists of members, subscribers, donors, or all three. The annual reports can contain information about the state of the organisation and whether it was satisfied with its progress, or indeed how it defined that progress. This will differ according to the type of organisation. Financial balance sheets will often appear in these printed reports.

There are also **newsletters**, produced weekly, monthly or quarterly and offering a more detailed picture of activities and functions. For example a church newsletter will often report on the state of the young people's club, the tennis club and bible classes. Local chambers of commerce may have produced lists of 'Prices Current' which detail the state of trade in the area.

Details of the membership of a local organisation can be used in a number of ways. For example the **admission records** of a friendly society—Foresters, Hibernians, Rechabites, Oddfellows, A.N.A., Protestant alliance, Sons of Temperance—will give you the date of admission of a member, his age and marital status. You can begin to understand something of the mobility of individuals and families, for admission records of a friendly society will often name the previous branch which has cleared the member and, when a member leaves a local branch, record his destination, unless he has not paid his dues!

In a similar fashion some **church records**, especially those of the Baptists and Congregationalists, will show whether a church member has been admitted by 'dismissal' or by testimony of faith. A letter of dismissal is a statement made by a clergyman attesting to the character and piety of an individual. These were presented to the minister of the new church and the membership records will sometimes give the location of the previous congregation. When church members leave a congregation, their destination is often recorded. You will find that some people join other denominations, are expelled for unacceptable behaviour, or lapse in their religious practice.

Details of church members can be picked up in **communicant lists** or **records of pew renters**. It was a common practice in most Protestant denominations for a family or individual to reserve a place in church. Pew rents were an important source of church funds, but they also show how people saw themselves in relation to their church. Church members in one sense could be regarded as proprietors, with a material as well as a spiritual stake in the life of their church. The renting of a seat in church need not indicate regularity of church attendance: you may well find that church attendance figures were below the total number of pew renters. Nevertheless, pew rents tell us something about the way people saw their church. Some churches have preserved their receipt books for the payment of pew rents; the books give the amount of money each member was expected to pay for the privilege of reserving a seat. For the Roman Catholic Church and other groups for which pew renting was not the custom, subscription lists will need to be the main source of information on membership.

Many churches have preserved their **Sunday School records**. These can include not only the minute books of Sunday School committees, but also statistics of attendance and enrolment books. The admission and attendance registers of some of these Sunday schools can be a rich source of information. The register of St Phillip's Uniting Church in Geelong, originally a Primitive Methodist church, for example, lists the names and occupations of both parents and children. The ages of these children are also provided, and occasionally changes in the place of residence of these pupils are indicated. Because many churches operated schools in the colonial period, some of the records of these establishments have survived. The records of other affiliated groups such as the Young Men's Mutual Improvement Societies can also be found in church archives, as well as the records of the visits which clergymen made to parishioners.

The committee **minute books** of various groups will usually contain only brief references to decisions or the state of an organisation's affairs, but sometimes they can be rewarding. Notices and announcements will sometimes be pasted or pinned to the pages of these volumes, or the occasional piece of correspondence might lurk in the most unsuspecting place. If the historian is investigating the development of buildings, then the minute books and reports of trustees and building committees are essential reading.

Parliamentary Papers

As always the various printed government reports and inquiries published in the Parliamentary Papers are helpful. Statistical registers (see p. 102) supply information about Benevolent Asylums, charitable organisations, public libraries, school and church attendance figures. Sometimes the information is quite brief, with some figures for expenditure, donations and staffing. Yet this may be just the material you require to fill the gaps in your study. The petitions of various groups in the community to colonial governments can be valuable in outlining some of the major issues of the period. The indexes to Parliamentary Papers list the petitions submitted to parliament (under the appropriate heading 'Petitions') and briefly describe the object of the petition and the people signing it. With little effort you can obtain permission to see the original petition. Petitions were required to be submitted to the Chief Secretaries' Departments if residents wished to establish local government in their locality. These can be found in the government gazettes, which are provided with indexes. On occasion the names of the petitioners are not included in the gazettes, but you should be able to find the original copy by using the registers to inward correspondence in a public record office.

Public record office files

The correspondence registers at a public record office can provide details about land grants for the purposes of religion or education. You can also read the correspondence of the local organisations seeking grants for building funds. These will often detail certain blocks of land in your local area which were allocated for public purposes—the friendly society's recreation reserve, the public park or botanical gardens. School building files often include a list of names of those people petitioning for the establishment of a school and also certain details about the number of families in the locality with children of school age. You should also be able to obtain the reports of local school inspectors which refer to educational standards, the abilities of teachers and the state of the school building. Reports of the various boards of education and their correspondence files will throw light on the activities of local school boards and their difficulties. Because the various colonies and States passed legislation on schools and their administration at different times, it would be wise to read a general text on the development of education in your state so that you can grasp clearly the various regulations affecting the building and administration of educational establishments.

Keeping records

The condition and completeness of any set of records which has once been maintained by a local organisation, whether it be the local church, fire brigade, library or football club, depends on the officials and a good deal of luck. Records have often been destroyed when a group moves premises. They can be destroyed or badly damaged through accident—fire, water (from a raging torrent to a leaking basement water pipe), or by deliberate design. They can be 'lost', that is, stored in a place which nobody can now recall, passed into the private possession of old members, or end up on the town rubbish heap. On the other hand they can be lovingly preserved by a historically minded secretary or church member, even to the extent that they may be catalogued and carefully organised in a trunk, cupboard or safe. Many such collections have found their way into the hands of local historical societies or manuscript collections in State libraries. Disappointments and surprises are part of the historian's experience; all one can do is try to exhaust all the possibilities in order to track down the material, and by individual effort try to convince people that local records of any sort have a value in local and, indeed, the wider society. This may help prevent the destruction of historical records in the future. The value of any sort of historical material depends, of course, upon the objectives of the researcher. All we have done here is suggest something of the variety and possible uses for these records.

4

Buildings

More than anything else, surviving buildings of an era long past can stimulate our imagination and interest in the life of earlier generations. Whether it be the awkward hut of a furrowed selector, the suburban terrace of a waistcoated tradesman, or the ornate mansion commanding a view of the pastures of the squatter or successful financier, our questions usually lead us into wider areas, and unless the historian considers some of these issues, population change for example, the particular construction and position of buildings may not be fully appreciated. The houses and buildings which surround us are the result of a multitude of decisions made by a variety of individuals and institutions: surveyors, local governments, speculators, landlords, prospective home owners and tenants. The character and location of these dwellings in turn relates to transport routes, local industry, the availability of building materials and the income and size of families. In this chapter we will explore some of the ways you can find and use information about the houses in the area of your interest.

BIOGRAPHY OF A STREET

Preston Street is situated in an area known as 'Ashby' in what is now the suburb of Geelong West. Today it is a residential street which includes houses both old and quite new in their building styles, and the subject of investigation under the auspices of the Geelong West Timber Museum Project. How can we learn of its development? It is best to begin at the beginning, and that means, if possible, the first parish **map** showing the sections and allotments surveyed before any land auctions were held (see p. 35). Of course, street names can change, and to be sure of things it would be wise to contact your local council or shire office for information on alteration in street names. For-

21a/b   These houses photographed in Preston Street in 1984 date back to the 1850s.

tunately, Preston Street has always been Preston Street. A parish plan, obtained from the State Library of Victoria, locates it in Allotment 5 of Section 1 in the Parish of Moorpanyal and tells us that this government allotment was bought from the Crown by Frederick

Griffith. In area it was 23 acres (9.3 hectares), bounded on the east and west by two roads laid out by the government, but having no others. Therefore the street is the result of private land subdivision, and the street will emerge when the owner either divides this land himself or sells it to others to subdivide.

The earliest map we can find for the Geelong West area which provides street names is one published in 1854. This does not mean, however, that Preston Street first appears in 1854. Remember that the street is our reference point only because in this case (and for most townships) it is the street which defines the location of dwelling places. This need not always be so, and in fact houses and other buildings can appear where no regular transport and service routes were established. But for our purposes the name of the street will help us find the houses we want. We now consult an early rate book and directory of the area. Geelong was incorporated as a municipality in 1849 and the first rate book was compiled in 1850. However, no streets are identified in this early rate book for the western part of the town. The only information telling us where people are living is the description 'Ashby', which is hardly satisfactory for our purposes.

The next best place to look is in a **town directory**. A search of the 1847 Port Phillip Directory again gives us general locations such as 'North Corio' or 'Geelong'. It is quite understandable in this early period, when Geelong's population amounted to less than 2000 people, that the town area would not be well developed and only the main streets and commercial centre of the town would be laid out. The NSW census of 1846 does tell us, however, that there were 150 people living in the area known as Ashby. By 1851 the population of the western area of Geelong, which included Ashby, had risen to 2607. It is between these two dates, 1846 and 1851, that we should expect much land to be subdivided and many building allotments sold. After the 1847 directory, the next directory is one published in 1851. This lists occupiers of houses, shops and farms in an alphabetical sequence. Checking through the names we find six people listed as living in 'Preston Street, Shirley Estate'. The researcher now has a fix on Preston Street. The name 'Shirley Estate' suggests that this is the section of the original government allotment which has now passed into private hands for subdivision. It is also evident to us that, given the twin names of the area, much of the land on the estate remains to be sold.

In many cases, directories are selective in the way they list residents of local areas. Often these directories were published with the aid of subscriptions from local businessmen and are not necessarily complete. Directories are often divided into sections. These will usually provide a list of business proprietors under appropriate descriptive headings such as 'Grocers' and 'Blacksmiths'. A section usually called the 'Street Directory' will list residents by the order of street names. Be cautious in the use of these documents. If your objective is to trace the development of a small area or sheet then the directory is often not a reliable source. For example, a count of the number of residents in Preston Street, using a directory for 1861, shows 29 people. Using the rate book the number of householders amounts to forty-three.

The **rate book** is the most systematic record of properties you will find. It is a record of the money levied on the value of the land and buildings by the local council and paid by the owner or resident. Old rate books, in varying states of repair, may be still held by the current shire or city council, or they may be held by a neighbouring council which was the original administrative body before some severance occurred. This is where your homework on changes in local government boundaries is needed. Some councils have given their records to the State archives. A rate book can give you information about the occupier and owner of the property together with a description and statement of its rateable value. The early Geelong rate books do not list the occupation of the resident, nor do they give us the name of the owner if he is not the resident. In the first half of the nineteenth century, two sets of records were kept: the rate book and the valuation or assessment book. Generally the valuation book lists owners and the rate book the residents.

Rate books can be used in conjunction with the local directory, the latter expanding the information about the occupations, and hence the livelihoods of the inhabitants. By using the rate book, two of the people listed as living in Preston Street in 1851 directory are located. Edwin Williams, a labourer, lived in a brick house of two rooms. The description reads 'Brick skilling 2r'. The word 'skilling' is a variation of 'skillion', a term used to describe a structure with a flat or sloping roof added to the rear or side of a building. This would usually contain a kitchen or small washing area. The other resident was Charles Chamberlain who also occupied a brick house with two rooms. In 1852 there were seven houses in the street, most being of the two-room type. There are, however, two houses of four rooms each, one of these was occupied by John Mahoney, a carpenter, who was paying £10 per year in rates. With one exception, a slab hut, all the dwellings in the street were made of brick. How typical was Preston Street in this respect? It is here that census figures from the local area can give us a guide and tables such as the one below compiled:

Table 6   Materials used in buildings of Ashby, Geelong, Victoria

	Brick and stone	Weatherboard, lathe and plaster	Total
1846	8	25	33
1851	306	206	512
1861	522	1110	1647

Source: W.H. Archer *Statistical Register of Victoria from the Foundation of the Colony* Melbourne, 1854; census of Victoria for 1861.

This table shows that brick and stone buildings outnumbered houses made from other materials in the 1850s and suggests that Preston Street conformed to the general pattern.

The table also shows that the number of houses in the area as a whole tripled between 1851 and 1861. The period was one of massive migration to the Australian colonies because of the discovery of gold, and the port towns of Melbourne and Geelong experienced dramatic population growth. With the growth of population came a demand for goods, services and, of course, houses. The comments of observers of the period can help give us an impression of the pace of change in the local scene. With civic pride, newspapers in 1854 reported on the expansion of the Ashby area:

> The progress of this portion of Geelong is rapid and bewildering. A little while ago it was a mere suburb, now it is an integral portion of the town, and its prime rates equal in value the best properties in Geelong. Large stores stand upon grounds which a few months ago was green sward, and whole streets are called into being so fast, that one is justified in believing that Aladdin has taken lodgings in the neighbourhood and has been busy rubbing his lamp.

It is in 1854 that we see from the rate book the population of Preston Street expand considerably. There are now sixteen houses in the street, and we can, by matching the names of earlier residents with the descriptions of their houses, begin to pinpoint these new houses. Now almost all of the new buildings are made of wood, and most contain two rooms. This change of material is surprising, and the explanation may lie in the relative costs and availability of brick and timber—but that is a side issue for the time being. In these early years houses were not given numbers, so it is difficult to make up an accurate map of the development of the street if we are tracing the houses *forward* through time, as we are at present. In a later part of this chapter a method of tracing houses *back* from a later point in time will be discussed. By using the names of the occupants and making allowance for those who have moved from the area, we can identify most of the new buildings. For example:

1852 Rate Book		1854 Rate book	
BUILDING	OCCUPANT	BUILDING	OCCUPANT
		BK 2R	Boulger, Martin
BK 2R	Flanders, George	BK 2R	Flanders, George
BK 4R	Hughes, James	BK 4R and Kitchen	Hughes, James
BK 4R	Barnes, William		
		W/b 2R	Barrett, Benjamin
		W/b 2R	Cooper, Benjamin
		W/b 4R	Bennett, Benjamin
BK Skillion	Sykes, Matthew	BK 2R	Sykes, Matthew
		W/b 2R	Pike, Joseph
BK Cottage	Mahoney, John	'Shirley Inn' W/b 12R	Mahoney, John
		W/b and shop W/b 1R	—— Steedman, William
BK 1R	Chamberlain, Robert	BK 2R	Chamberlain, Augustus
Slab 2R	Williamson, John	W/b 2R	Williamson, John
		W/b 2R	Martin, William
		W/b 2R	Nangle, George

Comparing these two lists, certain changes from 1852 to 1853 are immediately noticeable. James Hughes has added a kitchen to his house and Robert Chamberlain's wooden dwelling has another room. In addition to these points, we can see that Preston Street was becoming diversified. Together with the new houses, there is a shop and a hotel containing twelve rooms. Two things about the hotel are interesting. First, it is called the 'Shirley Inn', an indication that the name of the original land subdivision (the Shirley Estate) persisted. Second, the hotel was run by John Mahoney, the carpenter who a year earlier was occupying a brick cottage on the same block. He had probably built the hotel himself. His property was now valued at £500, quite a startling increase on the £10 of his house the year before. A change in the description of a building does not always mean an alteration in the actual building. For example, the house of Matthew Sykes is described in 1852 as 'a brick skillion of two rooms', while in 1854 the rate collector chooses to describe it as 'brick with two rooms'. There is no reason for us to expect that anything has changed except perhaps the rate collector describing the building. Moreover, rate collectors and other local officials were not always consistent in their manner of recording things.

The **valuation books** for Geelong begin in 1855, so we can now track down the owners of the properties in Preston Street. There are now 29 buildings where there were sixteen the year before. Among these are four shops, two tradesmen's workshops, a timber yard and the Shirley Inn. Fully half of the houses were owned by the people who occupied them. A comparison of the valuation books over a period of time draws attention to the way in which some individuals have increased their wealth. Charles Chamberlain, one of the original residents who made his living then as a ginger-beer manufacturer (not as prestigious as it might sound) was working as a carter and owned three houses in Preston Street in 1856.

The rate and valuation books can also tell us something about the building process and the quality of the houses in the locality. In the 1850s a conscientious rate collector in Geelong wrote comments on the condition of many of the buildings. It appears that Charles Chamberlain's tenants were not living in the best of dwellings as we find the note 'very bad' written beside two of his houses. A three-roomed weatherboard house built in 1853 is described as 'going to ruin' three years later. And John Mahoney's Shirley Inn, built in 1854, is judged as 'very inferior' by 1856. The speed of construction was evidently not matched by good workmanship in the gold-rush period. Nevertheless in the absence of building regulations construction still continued in Preston Street. The 1856 valuation book shows that there were five houses, all owned by James Parkinson, in the process of being built. In the words of the rate collector, 'wood frame and roof only up'. In the following year, the rate collector makes the note that Parkinson's houses were 'unfinished—not likely to be finished'. Sure enough the unfinished houses have disappeared from the rate book of the next year and Parkinson has left the area. Perhaps the house frames were used by local residents for firewood, or dismantled by Parkinson and sold to tradesmen in the town. The years 1857–58 were years of economic recession in Victoria, and it is likely that Parkinson was one of the victims. Preston Street was not doing well in these years, and the rate books show that many houses were empty.

Putting all these ingredients together and trying to visualise Preston Street with some imagination and without distorting our available evidence, what would we find, say, in 1855? We would be assailed at first by the smell of boiling animal fat from the small soap and candle factories nearby. Nevertheless the wheeze of bellows and clang of metal tempts us to venture down the street to William Hunter's forge, dodging potholes and the horse dung, with its own peculiar fragrance, as we go. The glow of fire and shooting sparks have attracted some other spectators also. There is not much to keep the children within those paling shacks whose walls, lined only with hessian and newspaper, barely keep out the summer flies or winter squalls. Further on the other attraction is the grocery store of Richard Coombs, but here's a dray approaching in a cloud of dust, its driver no doubt wishing he could join the good-natured joshing at the Shirley Inn. We make good our escape down a track scuffed through the tussocky paddock which separates two rows of the cottages abutting Preston Street, and so come to the main road.

TRACING INDIVIDUAL BUILDINGS

Notable buildings, like notable people, have already attracted attention and research. The results, in documented and illustrated volumes of 'historic houses' are available for the price of a good dinner. Some of these fine old buildings are open to viewers to wander through—approving the wide staircase, admiring the refurbished nursery and thanking heaven for the advances in kitchen design. There are also general books on early timber buildings, primitive architecture, station outbuildings, lacy suburban terraces, and so on, as well as the tourist-oriented, specially designed villages which recreate the past, like the mining village at Coal Creek, Korumburra, with old houses carefully shifted to the site and restored. The current fashion for the real estate sections of newspapers to review the past of a house they are featuring in their For Sale columns is another indication of interest in the history of individual buildings. However, the building you are likely to be interested in may well be none of these, and to trace its background, you probably have to start from scratch, and this may well mean working back through a rate book rather than forward as for a street biography.

To trace a house back through time using these records, extra information is also important, particularly the details of neighbouring buildings. A convenient way to begin your search is to find the rate book where street numbers are first used. In Geelong, for example, houses are numbered in 1900. Using the number of the house of interest, the local historian can then begin to search through earlier rate books, year by year, to trace the house. Note down all the details of your building, including the number. As you proceed back through the rate books you will find that the street number will not be included, so you need to juggle the other information to compensate for changes in the owner, occupier, number of rooms in the house, and the neighbouring houses and their owners. You should be able to keep track of the building even when owners and occupiers change. The following list demonstrates the process of dating:

8 McNicol Place			
Description	*Occupier*	*Occupation*	*Owner*
1900 Brick & w/b 6R	G. Skillen	Labourer	Andrews, Charles
1899 Same description	P. Haddon	Smith	Andrews, Charles
1898 Same desc.	Ann Vipond	—	De Groot, Henry
1898	same as above		
1890 Brick 6R & cellar	Alexander Duff	Labourer	De Groot, Henry
1888 Brick 6R	Wm Harrison	Bootmaker	P. Mulhair
1887–86	same as above		
1884 Same description	Charles Lock	Chemist	P. Mulhair
1880 No description	Empty		D'Arcy (agent)
1879 Brick 6R	William Downs		P. Mulhair
1878 Same description	Wray, Thomas	Draper	P. Mulhair
1877	same as above		
1876 Brick 6R	Charles Mead	Accountant	P. Mulhair
1875–74	same as above		
1873 Brick 6R	Wm Kingsbury	—	P. Mulhair
1872 Brick 4R & Kitchen	Charles Watson	—	P. Mulhair
1870–64	same as above		
1863 Brick 4R	John Wood	—	P. Mulhair
1862–61	same as above		
1860 Brick 4R	Henry Biggs	—	P. Mulhair
1859 Brick 4R	Richter, Henry	—	P. Mulhair
1858 Brick 4R (unfinished)			P. Mulhair

As can be seen in the final (in this case the earliest) entry, this house can be identified as having been built by 1859, although it was obviously extended between 1872 and 1873. The process is not always as simple as this, especially if the rate collector does not say whether rates are being paid on an unfinished house, or partly built house, or merely fenced land. The tracing list above shows how important it is to take account of changes in *owner, occupier*, and *dwelling description*. For example, from 1873 to 1872 only one of the identifiers used has remained constant. That is the name of the owner, P. Mulhair. The description of the house has changed, from a brick six-roomed house in 1873 to a brick four-roomed house in 1872. The names of the occupiers have also changed. You can see that had we not been taking account of the *owner's name*, we may have concluded that the house was either not there or we may have given up in despair. When the owner's name has changed, from 1890 to 1888 for example, we switch to using the description of the house as a linking point, although this is less reliable as there are obviously lots of four-roomed brick houses around and they are less distinguishable than people. Of course, it is also true that 'the owner' may also be 'the owner' of more than just one house. Then, if all of these variables change at once in a year, the researcher is really in strife and must make informed guesses on the basis of other evidence.

This is where the surrounding houses, their owners and occupiers, become important in tracing an individual dwelling. The example below demonstrates the importance of recording neighbouring buildings. The house in the middle is the one being traced.

1900	W/b 5R	Schweitzer, Wm	Householder	Schweitzer, Wm
	*W/b 6R	Field, Wm	Painter	Field, Wm
	W/b 3R	Betts, Edith	Householder	Baxter, John
1895	W/b 4R	Schweitzer, Wm	Householder	Schweitzer, Wm
	*W/b 5R	Johnson, Henry	Carpenter	Johnson, Henry
	W/b 3R	Carlson, Mary	Householder	Carlson, Mary

As you can see, the house of our interest is identified not through its own details but because one of the neighbours has remained, even though the neighbour, in this case William Schweitzer, has added a room to his own house. By listing both of the neighbouring houses, the historian has a better chance of identifying the changes occurring at his main focus.

When you start tracing houses from rate books you will see that these buildings develop in different ways, and this in turn can reveal some important facets of the building process and the relationships between houses and their occupiers or owners. For example, the writer traced two neighbouring houses owned and occupied by people sharing the same surname, Jacob Thewlis and Henry Thewlis. The properties were traced to a point where the rate book entry read: 'Fenced land 117 feet × 132 feet.' The land was owned by Jacob Thewlis, an ironmoulder. In the following year, 1890, Jacob built a five-room weatherboard house. Two years later another house appeared in the rate books. It was occupied by Henry Thewlis, a painter. We can conclude from this information that Jacob had bought the land, built his own house, and then built another house on the same block. With a surname as unusual as that, one could be excused for claiming Henry as a likely relative of Jacob.

22 Four houses remain in 1984 of the original six built by Baxter and Sons in Coquette Street.

In another exercise a row of four identical houses in Coquette Street, West Geelong, was traced using the rate books. Because the owners were the same in all cases, it was easier to track down these houses. As you can see from the rate book excerpts reproduced on p. 133 it would appear that 'Baxter and Son' were speculators: they were building houses not for themselves but for others to rent. While the houses are identical in appearance, the dates of their building are not the same. The first house (number 32) was erected in 1891. The next was built in 1892, and the other three dwellings were erected in 1894.

LIVING CONDITIONS AND LIFESTYLES

Investigating houses must lead to wondering about the people who fought, loved and dreamed in them. How did they live? It may be best to begin your enquiry by asking yourself some elementary questions about the place in which you live. What sort of functions do the various rooms serve? Where do you or your family spend most of your time, and for what purpose? Work, leisure and rest are three broad groups in which you can list your activities. How is your house current house numbers

Occupier		Occupation	Owner	Building description	
1895–96					
W Atkinson	John	Gardener	Everett Charles	" 6 Ro.	41
5 Baird	Robt Leslie	Smith	"	" 6 Ro.	18
6 Chapman	Edwd H.y	Saloon	Proctor, John	" 5 Ro Bar BR. 28	17
7 Boynton	Henry	Rayhhploy	"	" 5 Ro Stn BR. 30	16
8 Gee	Alfd Henry	Foreman	"	" 5 Ro Par BR. 32	16
Marshall Hay	John		"	" 5 Ro 10 Par BR. 34	18
1510	Leslie		"	" 5 Ro Stn BR. 36	17
1 Shire	John	Rayhhploy	"	" 5 Ro Par BR. 38	17
2 Armstrong	Bernard George	Carpenter	Polley John	" 6 Ro.	16
3 Wattson	Meany	Householder	Watsonton	" 3 Ro.	10
4 Johnson	Meany	Sailoress	Abraham James	" 4 Ro.	12

1892–93

1890–91

23 These exerpts from the Geelong West rate books illustrate the process of tracing houses back to the time when they were first built. Here the houses at Coquette Street are traced from the earlier to the later date. Note how important it is to keep referring to neighbouring houses and owners.

24 The bush photographer, woodcut from the *Australasian Sketcher* 1883. The selector's family is being photographed by a roving photographer. Note the head rests designed to keep the head still, and the toy trumpet used by the photographer to capture the attention of the child. National Library of Australia.

heated? How do you store your food? Wash your clothes? Once you are aware of these activities you can begin to study the past with a little more direction. You will quickly realise that much of what we may take for granted—sewerage, hot water, indoor toilets, built-in cupboards—just did not exist for the great majority of the Australian population, at least until the last decades of the nineteenth century. The point is made graphically by Hal Porter in his *Bairnsdale: Portrait of An Australian Country Town* (Sydney: J. Ferguson, 1977, p. 99):

> There are scores and scores of photographs of Victorian and Gippsland settlers taken by itinerant photographers during the late-1850s and after, photographs of family groups taken outside bark or shingle-roofed cottages. The bareness of the ground around the cottage, around almost every cottage so photographed, is what strikes one first—the grasslessness, the fact that there is not a plant. A tree? It is usually ringbarked, and makes its bleak and leafless comment.
>
> Use a magnifying glass on the men and women and children set up like

worn and awkward Noah's Ark figures in front of the slab or bark walls, still raw, uncompromising, uncontaminated by vine or creeper. Their hands are conspicuous, enlarged by labour, unused to graceful gesture, gothic lumps engrained with grime. Sunday best is worn: the women's feet hidden behind dust-sweeping skirts and layers of petticoats; the men in cardboard-stiff garments, slop clothes that have never been cleaned or pressed, each man with a black-finger-nailed hand splayed out in gauche elegance on one hip. You do not care to think of the state of their flannel underclothes, or when any of them last bathed, or if there is the luxury of a toothbrush somewhere inside the stark little building with its nose-door and eyes-windows. You prefer to avoid imagining what black gaps and decay-fretted teeth would be revealed if those grimly pressed-together lips could part. You shudder at the thought of what dreadful broth or hash simmers beside the unseen fire the smoke of which, never to disperse while the photograph lasts, can be seen creeping oilily out of the bark-and-boulder chimney. You hold a mental nose—God knows what they, the early settlers, smelt like.

Health reports

A good search through the indexes to the Parliamentary Papers of the colony or State relevant to your local area can turn up useful information in the guise of health reports, royal commissions and census figures. Many of these inquiries were concerned with matters of health and disease in urban areas and are often the only sources which give explicit evidence of working-class housing. Bear in mind that extreme cases are highlighted in their pages, as in this report of the Sydney City and Suburban Sewage and Health Board (1875):

> Garrett's Buildings (Clarence Street) contains ten houses, having two rooms each, 10 ft. by 10 ft., and 9 ft. high, rented for 6s. a week each; they are very badly ventilated, the back walls having no opening or air-hole of any kind. These ten houses occupy a piece of ground in the form of a parallelogram; five houses on either side with a space of 14 ft. in the centre. Of this 14 ft. space, 4 ft. 6 in. is fenced right and left and partitioned into yards for each house, leaving a passage of 5 ft.—exact measurement—down the middle, from end to end of the row as a thoroughfare ... But shocking to relate, this narrow passage which intervenes between the two rows receives all the drainage of the court, being nothing more or less than an open drain covered loosely with boards, not so effectually as to prevent the escape of foul gases, or with that object at all, but to allow the inmates of the house ingress and egress to their dwellings without breaking their shins.

Extreme or not, it still comes as somewhat of a shock to read the reports of central and local boards of health detailing some of the major problems associated with the local environment such as drainage, sewerage and water supply. In 1888 the Assistant Inspector of the Central Board of Health reported on a small country town. The summary read:

---

1 Population between 300 and 400 and is said to be increasing.
2 Water supply—from the B. Creek, and roof water.
3 Drainage—none.
4 Closets—a few pans; the remainder holes in the ground arrangement.
5 The roads are not metalled, few even formed.
6 Offensive trades—none.
7 Abattoirs—two slaughter houses, outside the town.
8 Swine—none kept in the town.
9 Scavenger—none.
10 Night soil depot—none.
11 The cemetery is situated above the town, and is within 150 yards of the bank of the creek.
12 Dairies are in the country.

This summary reveals a sad state of affairs but its headings indicate that it could have been much worse. Indeed the Inspector's gory account of his visit to the slaughterhouses makes one very glad they were 'outside the town'. Described in the body of the report is the small swamp on one town allotment which acts as a large cesspool for the nearby hotel, houses, Church of England and Mechanics' Institute. It was no surprise to find that when typhoid was diagnosed in 1889 in a visitor staying at the hotel, it soon swept the town, killing four people.

Housing reports

Before World War II, a number of State governments appointed boards to enquire into slum dwellings and substandard housing. Some of these, notably the reports of the Building Act Inquiry Committee of South Australia (1940) and the Housing Investigation and Slum Abolition Board of Victoria (1937), include detailed evidence about the size of rooms, number of people living in houses, sewerage, cleanliness and so forth illustrated by photographs.

Probates

From the accessibility of public official documents, it is rather a difficult step to the private documentation of probates and inquests which nevertheless can provide possibly the only evidence on individuals and their living conditions if public enquiries are not relevant. Probate is the legal process which sanctions the transmission of deceased estates, and probate files list the contents and value of a deceased person's estate. For the probate of a person's will (or letters of administration in cases where a will has not been made) to be granted, documents need to be lodged which contain an inventory of real and personal property with the values appended. Remember that not everyone who dies leaves property, and in some cases, depending on the laws of a particular colony or State, certain types of property—a small bank account or insurance policy—may not require the sanction of probate to be passed on to a person's family or nominated inheritors. But even if an estate is small, it may require probate if it contains a certain type of property, such as house or land. In the nineteenth century somewhere between 25 and 33 per cent of deceased adults left estates which were probated. Probate documents are indexed and these indexes are available at the various public record offices in State capitals. To track down the probate records of an individual you will need the date of that person's death. In most cases, the probate number will also be the number of that person's will, if he or she left a written record.

The details of assets and liabilities contained in these files vary quite considerably. For example the property of John Cahill, an engine driver, includes a weatherboard house of four rooms on land measuring 33 feet by 157 feet, an insurance policy worth £272 and furniture and clothes valued at £32. This does not tell us what type of furniture it was, or what sort of clothes he wore. In other cases you will find more detail, especially for those people who were comfortably off. Here is a list of the personal property of James Cowie, a retired gentlemen living with his daughter in Elsternwick, Melbourne.

Bookcase	£12/10/–
Books	£10
Pigeon holes	£1/10/–
Five pictures	£1/10/–
Bookshelves	10/–
Bedstead and clothes, commode	7/–
Set of drawers	5/–
Desk	£1
Watches and jewellery	£106
Money in hand	£14

Inquests and official records

Coroner's inquests, convened in order to discover the facts about deaths in violent or traumatic circumstances, produce transcripts of depositions given at the time. Inquest documents include both a medical report and the statements of people present at the time of death, or those thought to have relevant information. Because witnesses were required to inform the jury as fully as possible about their activities and observations, the transcripts of their evidence taken on oath before a jury can provide the historian with snippets of information. Like the probate material, the inquest documents are indexed both by year and in alphabetical sequence within the chronological breakdown. The following selections from inquest depositions give some idea of the potential of this source.

> I knew the deceased nearly two months, they lodged with us till yesterday when they moved to their own house.
>
> I found my wife in the room and she returned with me to the parlour. I was playing the violin, my wife was sitting on a chair, appeared in good spirits and health and asked to play a tune, making some complimentary remarks.
>
> I knew the deceased H—— C——, she was my servant and had been with me three months. She was in good health previous to the middle of Thursday evening. She slept with my eldest little girl in a house apart from the one I live in.
>
> The deceased ... has been living with me during the past three months, she rented a room from me.
>
> The house is of palings and cold.
>
> I heard the mother of the deceased through the wooden walls of the house say ... that [the baby] was eighteen months old.

With a collection of vignettes such as these you can begin to fit the pieces of the past together, incomplete as they may be individually. For a start you can deduce that it seems a common practice for individuals and families to rent rooms. In the case of the first excerpt the family was lodging with another family before settling in their own house. A search through the rate books revealed that the house consisted of just two rooms. Privacy was something that one could not expect in these small dwellings. The second excerpt suggests the existence of homemade music in the household. The third selection tells us something about the relationship between domestic servants and the families for whom they worked. The formal division between servants and their employers, which could be indicated by the presence of separate servants' quarters, was not a universal phenomenon. The fourth piece of evidence can be added to the first, in showing the frequency of room renting. Finally the fifth and sixth selections can be used to gauge the quality of some of the houses. Split palings were used for the cheapest of dwellings, and they were often not provided with lining, such as lathe and plaster. Usually of inferior timber, paling houses would quickly deteriorate, leaving little protection from the wind, rain, or (as we see in the last quotation) the personal affairs of neighbours.

Within this category of official records we can also include birth and death certificates. On occasions an individual's death certificate, for example, will indicate in whose house that person died. You may occasionally find in that section of the certificate allotted for the witness's name, something like this: 'Angus McIntyre, Labourer, Duneed, Son of deceased in whose house he died', or 'died in brother-in-law's house'. This sort of evidence can add to our understanding of the composition of the household, that is, the extent to which aged mothers, fathers or relatives' families shared the home with married children, brothers or sisters. With the help of birth registers the researcher can determine the number of people in a family at a particular time, and by finding information about their dwelling from rate books can come to some judgments about living conditions—how many were likely to have shared each bedroom, for example.

Local newspapers

Local newspapers, particularly in small towns, as usual have much to offer. If you do not have the time to spend long hours poring over the pages, head straight for the dates of foundation stones and openings, if you know them, of prominent buildings. Prominent buildings include not only churches, schools and banks but almost anything from a doctor's house to a bandstand. New enterprises—a flour mill, cordial factory, dairy or store, will often draw forth an article detailing precisely how the whole system works with an emphasis on its convenience and modernity. It is possible to trace all phases of a building through a newspaper: the initial advertisements for tenders with perhaps the names of architect or builder, general reports on the progress of the structure, the laying of the foundation stone, the official opening, subsequent additions or extensions, delays in the construction through industrial unrest or commercial depression, and perhaps disagreement among trustees over building design or lack of funds. Other occasions to look for are fires; accounts here list shop by shop as they were engulfed, or room by room if it is the local hotel in flames. And, of course, the new edifices are described as the rebuilding begins in the months to follow. Important visitors may mean a description of the main street titivated for the occasion.

Even skimming the paper for the time in which you are interested will bring forth many small bits and pieces of information. Auction notices can provide furniture lists of those people who are insolvent, leaving the area, or who have died. Sale notices and property descriptions help define the more prestigious locales: 'panoramic outlook', 'hygenic situation', 'opposite the residence of Doctor Shaw'. Where people choose to live, or where they are forced to live, suggests ways people are identified in a community. The relationships between residential areas and topography and the proximity of residences to economic activities are important, for they can help explain the size and cost of building allotments. Reports of court proceedings can reveal much about neighbourhood relationships (such as the woman taken to court by her neighbour who objected to her emptying slops in the street), the treatment of domestic servants, and so on.

Contemporary material

Overseas books provided a convenient guide or 'pattern' for the colonial builder or a client anxious to keep up with the Joneses in the northern hemisphere. One such influence on domestic building and some small industries was J.C. Loudon's *An Encyclopedia of Cottage, Farm and Villa Architecture*, first published in London in 1833 and reissued several times over the next 50 years. Trade and exhibition catalogues contain much detailed information and, as their value becomes appreciated, will be easier to find; a catalogue of furnishing and hardware put out by the Melbourne firm of James McEwan & Co. in the late nineteenth century has been reprinted.

Personal reminiscences

For general descriptions of houses and interiors, the old standby must be tried again—published diaries and individual memoirs, particularly of women, but not exclusively so. Here are some extracts from *The Letters of Rachel Henning* (Penguin, 1969), the correspondence of a woman who migrated to Australia, and eventually married and settled in Queensland:

> I have been doing a great deal in the preserving line lately. Last week we sent the storekeeper with a packhorse up the river and he got fifty dozen peaches for about 7s. I made about thirty-five dozen into jam, and the rest we kept for pies and eating. All hands helped at the jam. Mr. Somerville and Mr. Taylor peeled the peaches while I cut them up. Then Mr. Taylor and I alternately stirred the jam while Mr. Somerville cracked the stones that we might put in the kernels.

> ... we made an agreement with a carpenter to put up the house for us; that celebrated house which we have been so long planning. He agreed to do it more cheaply than we expected, which was very satisfactory. The house and kitchen, complete with doors, windows, floors, water pipes, boarded ceiling to the parlour, etc. will cost £115.

> The kitchen and servants' room is in a detached building, as is always the case in this country. The doors and window frames are to be of cedar. The house is twenty-four feet by thirty feet, with a verandah eight feet wide on three sides of it. It is to be finished in three months, then there is the kitchen and various outbuildings to be put up afterwards, so I do not suppose we shall get into it before the end of June or beginning of July.

Memoirs provide other helpful descriptions. A woman who grew up in the Sydney suburb of Bankstown during the 1890s recalled in *A Bunyip Close Behind Me* (Penguin, 1982):

> My sister and I were sleeping in the four poster in the second bedroom. The bed had been cut down and two hinged side wings added and draped with curtains of Nottingham lace. There was also a bolster and six feather pillows. So when the mosquito net was unleashed, the shutters closed, the transoms pulled to and the windows tightly shut, it's a wonder we were found alive in the mornings!

> In my day, everyone's dining-room walls were papered with embossed red paper, which must have been thought to stimulate the appetite. As in other rooms of the house, there was an elaborate overmantel above a funereal-black marble mantel piece, bearing the usual procession of things in regular formation. The side-board and dinner waggon sagged under silver covers, decanters, the tantalus, a colossal cheese dish and cruets on silver bases that spun round when you touched them.

There are also the published observations of travellers to Australia. Their opinions of life in the colonies are more often than not conditioned by their own social background, and because of this the historian needs to be aware of the selective nature of some of the information presented. Nevertheless, they can still offer entertaining glimpses of colonial life. Here is a selection of passages from Richard Twopenny's *Town Life in Australia* (Penguin, 1973), originally published in 1888:

Having seen the £600 a year cottage, it is almost needless to visit the £300 and £400, belonging to clerks and the smaller shopkeepers. The style is the same, but the quantity and quality inferior. For instance, the drawing-room carpet is tapestry instead of Brussels; the dining-room furniture is covered with horse-hair instead of leather, and so on. We will go into the next cottage—less pretentious-looking and a little smaller. The rent is twelve shillings a week, and it belongs to a carpenter in good employ. Here there is no drawing-room, but the parlour aspires to comfort quite undreamt of by an English tradesman. Our old friends the horse-hair cedar couch, the gent's and lady's chairs, turn up again. There is a four-foot chiffonier, a tapestry carpet, a gilt chimney-glass, a hearthrug, a bronze fender and fire irons, and a round table with turned pillar and carved claws.

These do not exhaust the possibilities for gaining information about houses and domestic life. The magazines and newsletters of local and state or regional historical societies often contain extracts from unpublished diaries or reminiscences of the older members of communities. Contact the historical societies in your local area as well as local libraries which may have collections of historical material. The manuscript collection of the state libraries in Australia include many diaries and reminiscences in unpublished form. James Hendy of Geelong wrote:

Mr. Oddie's 2 rooms were small and in order to economise room in the living room, the dining table was fastened to the wall with hinges so that it could be let down as a flap when not in use—this struck me as a novelty, I remember.

At least that would not be out of place in some of today's flats.

Appendix 1

Common Abbreviations

anon.	anonymous
app.	appendix
b.	born
© or c.	copyright
c. or ca	*circa*, about, approximately (used with dates)
cf.	*confer*, compare (advice to reader)
d.	died
ed., eds	editor, editors
edn	edition
e.g.	*exempli gratia*, for example
et al.	*et alia*, and others
et seq.	*et sequentes*, and following
f., ff.	following (one or more pages following the page given)
fac.	facsimile
ibid.	*ibidem*, in the same work
i.e.	*id est*, that is
loc. cit.	*loco citato*, in the place cited in previous footnote
MS	manuscript (plural, MSS)
n.	note, footnote
n.d.	no date of publication given
op. cit.	*opere citato*, in the work cited
p.	page
passim	here and there in the work cited
q.v.	*quod vide*, which see (a cross reference)
sic.	as in original quoted. (used in brackets to indicate error or unusual statement in a quotation)
ts.	typescript
vol., v.	volume

Appendix 2

Useful books

INTRODUCTION TO RESEARCH

Sir John Ferguson *Bibliography of Australia (1784–1900)*, Sydney: Angus & Robertson, 1941–69. 7 vols. Facsimile, ed. Canberra, National Library of Australia, 1975–77. (The standard reference for printed matter, 1874–1900)

D.H. Borchardt *Australian Bibliography: a Guide to Printed Sources of Information* Sydney: Pergamon, 1976

National Library of Australia *Newspapers in Australian Libraries: a Union List. Part 2, Australian newspapers* Canberra, 1975, 3rd edn. (Lists all known surviving newspapers by place of publication)

T. Hogan, A.T. Yarwood and R.B. Wood *Index to Journal Articles on Australian history* Armidale: University of New England, (guide to articles published in main scholarly journals until 1973; since updated by others)

National Library of Australia *Australian Public Affairs Information Service*, Canberra (A subject index to material appearing in articles and conference papers on the social sciences and humanities. Appears monthly—the best way to update other references)

Australian Society of Archivists Inc. *Our Heritage, a Directory to Archives and Manuscript Repositories in Australia* Canberra, 1984

J. Monie *Victorian History and Politics, European Settlement to 1939, a Survey of the Literature* Melbourne: La Trobe University, 1982. (A two-volume must for Victorians but also valuable for historians from other States as most chapters begin with Australia-wide references. See, for instance, chapters on general reference sources, military history, economic history, transport, education, religion, health and the press)

L. Stewart *Nineteenth century Australian periodicals: an annotated bibliography* Sydney: Hale & Iremonger, 1979

Directory of Pictorial Resources compiled by M. Davis and H. Boyce, Melbourne Centre for Environmental Studies, University of Melbourne, 1981

C. Flower *The Antipodes Observed: Prints and Printmakers of Australia, 1788–1850*, Melbourne: Macmillan, 1975

C. Tanre *The Mechanical Eye: a Historical Guide to Australian Photography and Photographers* Sydney: University of Sydney, 1977

J. Barzun and H.F. Graff *The Modern Researcher* New York: Harcourt, Brace Jovanovich, 1977, 3rd edn

Oral history Association of Australia Journal (Begun in 1978)

L. Douglas and P. Spearritt 'Talking History: the use of oral sources' in W. Mandle and G. Osborne (eds) *New History: Studying Australia Today*, Sydney. George Allen & Unwin, 1981. (Also useful for chapters on aboriginal history, women's history, communication, urban history, post war immigration)

L. Douglas and P. Spearritt *Australia 1938 Oral History Handbook*. (Contains bibliography, interviewing hints and the questionnaire for the Australia 1938 volume of the Bicentennial History)

LAND

J.M. Powell and M. Williams (eds) *Australian Space, Australian Time* Melbourne: Oxford U.P., 1975

Sir S.M. Wadham *Australian farming, 1788–1965* Melbourne: Cheshire, 1967

Sir S.M. Wadham R. Kent Wilson and J. Wood *Land Utilisation in Australia* 4th edn, Melbourne: Melbourne U.P., 1964 (1st published 1939, authors S.M. Wadham & G.L. Wood)

D.N. Jeans *An Historical Geography of New South Wales to 1901* Sydney: Reed, 1972

L.J. Peel *Rural Industry in the Port Phillip Region, 1835–1880* Melbourne: Melbourne U.P., 1974

G. Blainey *The Rush that Never Ended* 3rd edn, Melbourne: Melbourne U.P., 1978. 1st published 1963. (Useful bibliography on mining)

J. Birmingham, I. Jack and D. Jeans *Australian Pioneer Technology: Sites and Relics* Melbourne, Heinemann, 1979. (For agricultural machinery, mining, pastoral, maritime, timber industries and some crops)

W. Calder *Beyond the View: our Changing Landscapes* Melbourne: Inkata, 1981. (Synthesis of viewpoints of geology, geography, biology, climatology, etc., in approach to landscape as an interlocking, complex system of relationships)

D. Saunders (ed.) see reference under *Buildings* for title-searching procedures

---

PEOPLE

N. Gray *Compiling Your Family History: A Guide to Procedure* Sydney: Society of Australian Genealogists, 1981. 9th edn

E. Lea-Scarlett *Roots and Branches* Sydney: Collins, 1979

A.G. Puttock *Tracing Your Family Tree* Melbourne: Lothian, 1979 *Australian Dictionary of Biography*, vol. 1– . Melbourne, Melbourne U.P., 1966–

A Select Bibliography of Aboriginal History and Social Change: theses and published research to 1976 in *Aboriginal History*, vol. 1 (II), 1977

A.H. Pollard *Demographic Techniques* Sydney: Pergamon, 1974

E.A. Wrigley *An Introduction to English Historical Demography* London: Edward Arnold, 1966

C. Flower *Duck and Cabbage: A Pictorial History of Clothes in Australia, 1788–1914* Sydney: Angus and Robertson, 1968

M.M. Cannon *Australia in the Victorian Age* vol. 1, *Who's master? Who's man?* vol. 2, *Life in the Country* vol. 3, *Life in the Cities* Melbourne: Nelson, 1971, 1973, 1975. (Colourful social histories best used for extensive bibliographies of primary and secondary sources)

Finlayson, J.A.S. *Historical Statistics of Australia: a Select List of Official Sources* Canberra: A.N.U., 1970

BUILDINGS

D. Saunders (ed.) *A Manual of Architectural History Sources in Australia* Adelaide: University of Adelaide, 1981. Comprehensive coverage of whereabouts of field notes, archival material, picture collections, maps, publications and unpublished reports. Vol. 1: NSW and SA, with advice on using advertisements, directories, 'pattern books', sale notices and catalogues, tenders, and so on; vol. 2: Vic. and WA

R. Boyd *Australia's Home: its Origins, Builders and Occupiers* Melbourne: Penguin, 1968. 1st published 1952

M. Lewis *Victorian Primitive* Melbourne, Greenhouse, 1977

P. Cox and J. Freeland *Rude Timber Buildings in Australia* London: Angus and Robertson, 1980. 1st published 1969

P. Cox *Australian Colonial Architecture* Melbourne, Lansdowne, 1978

J. Birmingham, I. Jack and D. Jeans *Industrial Archaeology in Australia: Rural Australia* Melbourne: Heinemann, 1983

H. Tanner, P. Cox and others *Restoring Old Australian Houses and Buildings: an Architectural Guide* Melbourne: Macmillan, 1975

Illustrated Glossary of Architecture London: Faber & Faber, 1966. Many other dictionaries on architecture and building materials exist. Usually English terms were imported into Australia but a new or different term was often used in cases common in Australian building but not in Britain

Index